THE
SUSTAINABLE
SOCIETY

THE SUSTAINABLE SOCIETY

Ethics and
Economic Growth

ROBERT L. STIVERS

THE WESTMINSTER PRESS
PHILADELPHIA

BOOK DESIGN BY DOROTHY E. JONES

PUBLISHED BY THE WESTMINSTER PRESS®
PHILADELPHIA, PENNSYLVANIA

PRINTED IN THE UNITED STATES OF AMERICA

Library of Congress Cataloging in Publication Data

Stivers, Robert L   1940–
   The sustainable society.

   Includes bibliographical references.
   1. Economic development. 2. Economic development—
Moral and religious aspects. I. Title.
HD82.S836   338.9   75-40049
ISBN 0-664-24789-X

To S.K.S., L.A.S., and M.L.S.

Contents

Foreword
by ROGER L. SHINN

Modern mankind, more than most people realize, has tied its hopes to that immense burst of economic productivity that followed the Industrial Revolution.

Did affluent societies toy with the idea of a war on the poverty in their midst? They sought to finance the war from the "growth dividend" of the society rather than demand any radical sharing of wealth.

Did moderately generous people worry about the horrendous gap between the richest and poorest nations? The usual proposals were for economic development of the poor societies, often with the United States as something of a model for the world.

Did statesmen work toward the goal of reducing war? One of their main aims was increased productivity that would reduce economic discontent.

But suppose that the facts do not agree with the expectations. Then what?

Suppose that the major technological and economic achievements have increased the gap between rich and poor or the power of exploiters over exploited. Suppose

—if it is necessary to suppose—that starvation has increased despite the technical problems of the Green Revolution. Suppose, as some believe the case to be, that even the affluent are losing freedom to perplexing forces that shape history, decreeing simultaneous employment and inflation, dehumanizing social life, poisoning the air and water, and inflicting chaos on transportation of people from home to work—and in the process alienating many of the best youth from their societies.

Or suppose that hard evidence leads able thinkers to say that mankind is pushing the earth to the limits of its productivity. Suppose that the energy crisis and the hunger crisis and persistent inflation are part of an early-warning system, telling this human race that its exploitation of the earth's resources cannot continue to expand forever.

An impressive literature, most of it within a very few recent years, has made this case. Some experts are arguing that, just as mankind must sooner or later settle for Zero Population Growth, it must also settle for Zero Economic Growth. The slogan, like most slogans, is too simple. Some kinds of economic growth can continue; others, those that consume irreplaceable resources and pollute excessively, are more threatening. So a more accurate language refers to differential growth or suggests a dynamic equilibrium as an economic goal.

The implications of ending the type of economic growth that modern societies have come to want and expect are staggering. To sort them out requires an investigation of current controversies about technology, economics, politics, and ethics.

That is what Robert Stivers has done in this book. In a nondogmatic way he has looked into the arguments, moved back and forth across the lines of scholarly disciplines, acknowledged many uncertainties, yet made some firm judgments. He has concluded that our world needs every scientific and political skill that can be summoned to meet the challenges before it. Above all, he says, we need a new world view and a religious commitment that, for all its Biblical roots, must break with most inherited traditions.

To take Dr. Stivers seriously, as I think we must do, is to revise many of the classical debates about the ways to achieve social justice and a sustainable society. Traditional liberal capitalism and traditional Marxism alike assumed a continuing growth in production that now seems improbable or impossible.

Granted, nobody knows what prodigies of ingenuity may postpone troubles. Equally, nobody can count on continuous reprieve. Ethical responsibility thus requires a rejection of the customary comfortable thought that we can evade the hard decisions of social justice by expecting economic growth to spare us the pain.

Yet Dr. Stivers writes with a remarkable hopefulness. He shows that Christians may find in the judgments of God the promises of God. And he suggests that those who are willing to make tough decisions may find a way of life better than the deceptive attractions that now hold the world in their spell.

This book is for people who, because they take their faith seriously, want to act responsibly in the predicaments of our world.

Preface

Some years ago as an officer of the U.S. Navy I sailed through the Hellespont toward Istanbul. As I remember it, our ship was at the head of a column consisting of one aircraft carrier, two cruisers, and numerous destroyers. It was early in the evening, typically warm and clear as are all Mediterranean summer evenings. I was struck by the greenness of the land in the vicinity of ancient Troy, a greenness that stood in stark contrast to the denuded hillsides of much of the Mediterranean coast. It seemed so peaceful.

Yet not five miles from where I stood on the fantail of the ship, one of the famous battles of history took place. Perhaps it wasn't so titanic a struggle as the myths and legends would have us believe. Nonetheless, this beautiful countryside was once disturbed by the aggressions of human beings trying to wrest from other human beings an extra ounce of prestige, glory, and wealth.

Why are men so aggressive when they have such a garden to live in? Indeed, I asked myself what I was doing there at the head of a powerful armada, which by striking with just one of its many nuclear weapons could have reduced ancient Troy and the contending armies to nothingness. Hector and Achilles would have had no defense. As it was, we were at "peace" with the ground on which Troy stood. The only disturbance we created was the wash of our wake as it broke on the nearby beaches, the very beaches where once stood a gigantic wooden horse.

Somewhere along the way of this study I recalled that evening. The recollection brought back the tale of the Trojan horse. The Greeks deceptively built and used it and, because of the ideological blindness of the Trojans, they achieved a victory that brute force had been unable to win.

We are at once Greeks and Trojans. We are Greeks in that we continue to build our horses in the form of powerful machines embodying the latest technological "advances." The column of ships is just one example. We continue to use brute force. We continue to deceive ourselves and others. But what is our aim? Victory? Victory over what? Over the verdant countryside where Troy once stood? Over others, modern Trojans? What are we about in building our gigantic machines, in destroying the countryside, in subjecting ourselves and other people? Plainly and simply, we seem to be without purpose. We aimlessly sail our ships, unsure or not quite caring what lies over the horizon.

We are also Trojans. The Trojans were faced with the problem of what to do with the horse their kinsmen the Greeks had built. We are in their position. Our ancestors have left us a gigantic machine which our ideology tells us we must worship. What is our aim in dragging this machine to the center of our culture? Shouldn't we at least be a bit more prudent and careful as we drag it through the streets? We need to know what lies in the bowels of our machine. We need to seal shut that door in its side. We need to clean the dust and dirt of passage from its legs. We need to find a course through the gates and streets of our city that doesn't result in destruction. We need to go a bit slower to avoid running over people who get in the way.

A column of warships moved through the Hellespont one summer evening. Its weapons were aimed at peace. Or were they? Its direction was Istanbul. Or was it? Its builders and directors were aimed at material abundance. Or were they? Like that naval armada, we seem to be at a turning point. Something is radically wrong not only with our economic system, but with our lives. A deep sense of crisis dominates our consciousness. Yet we are immobilized. We cast about for direction, not sure where we are or where we should be going.

Now, some twelve years later, I have come to doubt received wisdom. Such doubt has led me not to despair but to hope. I have become aware that inherited economic systems and received wisdom about these systems, which exert a powerful influence on life, do not embody the meaning of life. The meaning of life is God's love in Jesus Christ. What, then, should we do with our Trojan horse? Obviously the answer is to reconceive it as a means, eliminating the alienating characteristics through which it has been turned into both means and ends. But above all else we need to come to a new awareness of the need for confession, repentance, new life, and action based on this new life. This will be no simple task, but responding responsibly to God's love never has been a simple task.

The debate over economic growth needs both sober, balanced analysis and prophetic criticism. The crisis is too deep, the direction too uncertain for us to proceed without the best information available. "Shooting from the hip" will solve nothing. But sober, balanced analysis smacks of the "old way." It tends to be a conservative approach that forces us to play in the ball park of the powers that be. Prophetic criticism must therefore enter. It has two tasks: to measure our analysis and actions against the plumb line of God's justice and to call us to confession, repentance, and new life.

My own sympathies in this study are on the side of a radically changed economic order. Objectivity has been impossible, but I have attempted to retain some semblance of balance by presenting opposing viewpoints. Indeed, I fear the prophetic voice is too restrained, but trust some will find it, however muted it may be.

Many deserve credit, but special mention must go to Roger Shinn of Union Theological Seminary in New York City, who provided helpful criticism in the early stages, and to Donna Dickason, whose superior skills saved me long hours. Also I must thank my colleagues at Pacific Lutheran University, who coaxed me through the final draft, and my family, who provided immense, though often intangible, support. Finally I am grateful to many helpful persons whose support kept me whole through the project.

R. L. S.

Tacoma, Washington

Chapter 1

THE GROWTH DEBATE

North America in the 1960's and 1970's is not the firmest of platforms for viewing the horizon. It is like a roller coaster, with the riders so caught up in the dips and curves that the horizon is a topsy-turvy blur.

We twist and turn from social unrest to quietism, from activism to "getting your own head straight"; yet injustice and conflict remain. No less confused, the economy gyrates from prosperity to inflation to recession; yet the stock market rises and luxury resorts are full. Oil is plentiful, then becomes scarce; yet we hear of gluts and production cutbacks. The government pays farmers to keep land out of production, while the newspapers are full of accounts of world famine. Still, farmers plow wheat under and slaughter livestock to keep prices up. Large families are encouraged (in the Associated Press photo, the Mother of the Year *always* had five or six children). Then we learn that the world is getting too crowded, so we cut back and change our attitudes. Even so we are told that one American equals twenty-five Indians in terms of environmental impact. And all the while day-to-day chores grab our attention. We get lost in the details. Exasperated, yet still concerned, we wonder—in the occasionally flat stretches of the roller-coaster ride—where it is all leading.

For one trying to assess the horizon from this unstable platform, even more exasperating is the disagreement among those whose profession it is to locate the horizon. To shift metaphors, it is as if we are the Trojans watching our experts try to evaluate wooden horses in our midst. Are the horses gifts from the gods or do they have enemy soldiers hidden within?

Of the many wooden horses in our midst, one is particularly troublesome. It is the many-sided phenomenon of growth. Growth has for some time been a priority-setting doctrine in the creed of industrial culture. This doctrine, along with unprecedented developments in science, technology, and social organization, has released an unparalleled amount of energy. The result is seen in an increasing population, in the spiraling consumption of material goods and services, and in the flowering of technical expertise. Until recently, nearly everyone looked on this expansion and outpouring of energy with satisfaction. It was desirable, both in itself and as means to other ends. The growth-horse was obviously a gift from the gods.

But now an increasing number of dissenters are raising a challenge. They are asking two probing questions. (1) Are present forms of growth, particularly rising population, the increasing pressure on resources, and the pervasive spread of pollution desirable? (2) Can these forms of growth continue much longer?

Some of these dissenters are predicting the collapse of the world's present industrial system because of the

combined pressures of too many people, too few resources, too much pollution, and a misdirected technological process. Others, unsure on the question of
collapse, are critical of the growth ideology. They view
with misgivings the way in which a significant portion of
the world's people have succumbed to a way of life
dominated by economic and technological considerations. Both of these groups claim that growth in many of
its present forms is a Trojan horse containing enemy
soldiers.

Nevertheless, expansion continues. It is pushed along
by material and ideological forces. It has many powerful
supporters. It may already have become an "irresistible
force."

Is growth in both its ideological and material forms a
Trojan horse? Has it produced a repressive culture that
neglects both nature and persons in the name of false
gods? Are certain forms of growth leading to ecological
collapse and the exhaustion of natural resources? These
are just a few of the questions over which the critics and
advocates of growth differ. Their differences are significant. It is not just an academic debate for the elite.
Repressive ways of living, mass starvation, foul air and
water, and economic collapse affect each of us now, and
offer the possibility of even more serious difficulty to our
children. The debate over growth is with us. It will
remain with us for some time and must be assessed in
spite of our roller-coaster platform.

Many ecologists, economists, and technologists have
commented on the questions at issue. A fairly impressive, though by no means adequate, body of evidence has
accumulated. Nevertheless, the broader ethical questions
as well as several more specific moral issues have not

been adequately treated. Indeed, the ethical and moral issues often have been neglected in favor of technical and political questions. Nor has the debate itself been evaluated from a Christian perspective.

The purpose of our exploration is twofold: to make a statement of the human prospect, and to probe from a Christian perspective the ethical and moral issues raised in the debate over growth. We will confine ourselves largely to growth in the more developed countries. We will not ignore the less developed countries, but we want to avoid the self-righteous syndrome of some white Westerners who take it upon themselves to lecture the rest of the world on "what you should be doing."

What can we say about the future from our roller coaster? Will it be a time of promise or a time of suffering and doom? For some in the debate, this is the most crucial question of all. For Christians, the future is a time of promise. Hope issues spontaneously from faith. But this does not necessarily mean that the future will be a time of material comfort. God does not promise material prosperity. God does not reward "the elect" with large fortunes and $75,000 homes. Nor is God the *deus ex machina* who will come in to set things right in the face of imminent human suffering. Men and women are free to defy God and to set up material prosperity as a golden calf.

Christians therefore are simultaneously hopeful and realistic about the human prospect. Hopeful, because God is and will be present with love in all situations, and his love has power to tap the unlimited store of human goodwill and cooperative action. Realistic, because we know much needs to be done by less-than-loving individuals and groups. But of the two, hope sets the basic

mood. God will be present in the future. We have that
assurance. God pulls and pushes us into the unknown.
He calls and prods us to ever higher realizations of love
and justice. We stand therefore not with a sense of
doom—which in the welter of conflicting assessments
may seem tempting—but with hope, no matter what the
material future holds in store.

Even so, an agonizing question remains. Will the
activity of God, the responsiveness of persons, and hope
proceeding from faith be sufficient to prevent widespread
human suffering? Here a resounding "Yes!" would be a
comfort. Unfortunately, this is precisely what we can't
offer. Moreover, it is the very reason the future is so
troublesome, the roller-coaster ride so dizzying. In all
honesty we must admit that we are free to defy God and
ignore the future. So while the basic mood and outlook
are hopeful, we must have no illusions. We are neither
optimistic nor pessimistic, but hopeful and realistic.

To probe the second part of our purpose, the more
specific ethical issues that confront us now, we must also
realize that God is active in the present. Past, present,
and future—God acts, in the words of theologian Paul
Lehmann, "to make and keep human life human."
Christian action is responsive therefore both to the loving
activity of God and to the needs of the neighbor. It does
not neglect the present for the past and future. It
responds with love to the situations that are presented
and in which God is certainly at work.

Nevertheless, attempts to locate precisely where God
is at work and what specific actions constitute an
authentic response of love are complicated and difficult.
In an age of high technology and complex social structures, situations and solutions are seldom "neat and

clean." Moreover, in our fallen condition we are never fully responsive either to God or our neighbor.

We are not without resources, however. Clues for what may constitute a loving response are available. The Bible, for example, is a record of God's activity and the response of believers. It tells us where God has been and points to certain activities as examples. It reveals a God who is unpredictable and free in the specific details, yet constant in love and justice.

Further clues can be found in the Christian tradition. In the long history of the church a wide variety of situations have been addressed with acts of Christian concern. Likewise, our own religious and secular communities offer resources. American and world church bodies, for example, have for some time been calling attention to personal and social problems in the midst of which God is almost certainly at work.

Nor can we overlook the personal work of the Spirit in each of us. Calling this or that inspiration or intuition the work of the Spirit has historically led to notorious injustice. Yet, as many Christians affirm, love actually creates a response in us. It is a response based in humility, sensitive to pride and error, and in complex social issues eager to be instructed by whatever intelligent resources are available. But it is a response that can be counted on. There is a fund of goodwill in each of us and to a degree in our social organizations.

In other words, Christians carry a lot of baggage into their reflection on social problems. This is not the place to unpack this baggage, for our primary purpose is not theological. Nevertheless, we should be clear that all this baggage, all the clues and guides available, do not, indeed cannot, make a decision for us or point infallibly to correct answers. They all are merely aids. However valid they may be in themselves, doctrines and laws are often ambiguous and sometimes in conflict in concrete situations.

But there is an even more fundamental reason to be cautious. The call to love and justice comes new and fresh in each situation. The cross and the resurrection free us from the law, from slavish adherence to clues, guides, norms, traditions, and whatever else may be used to inform ethical reflection. The gospel is the good news that we are free. We are free to respond with love, whatever the circumstances may be. Thus, Christians struggle with an armload of baggage, and it is right that they do. Yet they are alert to jettison the baggage in order to help others who have been "set upon by robbers." They are free for seeing a new situation with clarity.

Sometimes being alert to jettison baggage also means speaking a language understandable to non-Christians. Our age deals very little in either "God talk" or theology; yet it is possible to communicate. Christians and non-Christians share many values because of the pervasive historical influence of Judaism and Christianity. They also share many common experiences. And beyond the possibility of communication lies the necessity of it. If the problems associated with growth are as serious as some think, we cannot merely talk to ourselves.

Consequently our exploration will not include a detailed inspection of the Christian baggage. In most cases the theological assumptions will be obvious. We will not, however, always make these assumptions explicit, preferring in many cases to pursue a "public ethic" that speaks in terms familiar to a variety of communities.

Equally important to the theological perspective in the treatment of complex ethical problems is knowledge of the situation. What are the facts? What is going on? A theological perspective is not particularly helpful at this point. Much more significant is the ability to ferret out information.

Here arises a problem peculiar to recent history. "Information" has become increasingly complicated, largely because of science and technology. Simple problems with simple solutions do not often occur, especially when more than a few persons are involved. More and more, "information" is becoming the province of the expert scientist and technician.

Responsive ethical reflection requires both a basis for value judgments and a knowledge of the facts. Sound social policy must be technically efficient as well as morally acceptable. Ethics and the sciences are consequently converging activities. Increasingly both ethicists and scientists are recognizing the importance of dialogue in the shared task that alone can produce sound social policy and goals.

The scrutiny of the growth debate that follows is an attempt to combine insights from the natural and social sciences with a Christian perspective. Our intention is to use the combination as an instrument of criticism and construction. God judges and redeems. We must rigorously submit to judgment what has been, what is, and what is projected. Beyond judgment we must look toward the kingdom of God, toward new constructions of love and justice in response to God's redeeming grace.

In this process of criticism and construction we will pay particular attention to three arenas of activity. Social problems have structures that must be understood, their solutions inevitably have political repercussions, and criticism necessarily involves ethical judgments. Stated differently, our criticism and our constructive efforts must be attentive simultaneously to engineering, politics, and ethics. To neglect any one of these three leads to a truncated analysis and eventually to poor policy.

Attention to the Use of Words

One important structure to which we must give attention has to do with the use of words. What is meant by the word "growth"? When it is said that "growth" may be a Trojan horse, what growth is referred to? Certainly some forms of growth, for example, that of a child, are not in question. Neither is population growth the center of dispute in the debate over growth. The world's current population is approximately 4 billion. It is growing at an exponential rate of 2 percent annually and will reach 4.9 billion by the year 1985 and 7.7 billion by 2008, if the 2 percent rate is maintained. Virtually all observers concede the necessity of drastically reducing and eventually eliminating population growth. Heated disputes involving unresolved ethical questions rage over how best to accomplish this, but the goal itself is not at issue, except perhaps for some minority group spokesmen, such as Dick Gregory, who see racist motives in attempts to control population.

Economic growth is far more complicated. In the broadest terms, it includes the wide range of ideological and material factors that have produced the affluence and abundance of the industrialized countries. This definition, however, is neither common nor precise. It is better to refer to this wide range of factors as the "thrust for growth" and within that "thrust" to view economic growth as a more limited definition. This is not to imply, however, that this combination of ideological and material factors is insignificant. On the contrary, an understanding of the thrust for growth is critical to the debate.

The generally accepted and narrower meaning of the term "economic growth" is the increase of an economy's output of goods and services over a period of time. It is usually measured by an accounting device known as gross national product (GNP), adjusted to eliminate the distorting effects of inflation or deflation. In terms of GNP, economic growth is simply the annual increase of the economic system in monetary terms. The debate over growth is very much concerned with this form of growth and with GNP as its measure.

Still more complicated is the understanding of technological growth. In broad terms, participants in the debate equate technology with what Jacques Ellul calls "technique," that is, "the totality of methods rationally arrived at and having absolute efficiency (for a given stage of development) in every field of human activity." [1] In this sense, technological growth expresses the seemingly inevitable increase in rational planning and control characteristic of most industrialized societies.

Again, Ellul's "technique" is not precise enough. "Technology" and "technological growth" usually refer to a narrower process involving the production of goods and services. Ellul's contention, however, is much at issue in the debate. His term "technique" points to what may loosely be called the technologization of the human soul, the domination of all human activity by efficiency, planning, and production. It is a critical issue, yet this usage does not permit adequate scrutiny of certain productive technologies that observers such as Barry Commoner claim are the main cause of pollution.

Technology in the narrower sense is applying scientific knowledge to the practical problems of producing goods and services. Technological growth is the increase both in scientific knowledge and its utilization to solve problems. Even more precisely, technology is a process whereby increases occur in the units of output produced per unit of input. Technological growth in this sense means increasing productivity or efficiency and is frequently measured in terms of increasing GNP per man-hour.

Economic growth and technological growth are obviously not the same thing. Yet they are closely linked. Economist Edward F. Denison, in a detailed study of the factors that have contributed to economic growth in the United States during the period 1929–1957, has established that approximately 32 percent of the increase was attributable to increased productivity.[2] In fact, economic and technological growth are mutually reinforcing. The relationship is so close that it allows us to use the less cumbersome terms "economic growth" and "economic process" to refer to what in reality is a much more complex amalgam of economic, technical, and other material factors.

The economic process, as presently constituted, results in other forms of growth. Two are notable in the debate: the growth of pollution, and the increasing quantity of raw materials used in manufacturing. These forms of growth are largely self explanatory. The question is: Are they mere side effects or an intrinsic part of the growth process? Is it possible to have ever-increasing production of material goods without ruinous pollution and depletion? In short, can economic growth continue?

Some critics of growth simply say that economic growth cannot continue. In strict terms this is not correct. What such critics are in fact saying is that forms of growth in which pollution and depletion are intensive cannot continue. Obviously there are some forms, most services for example, that have no physical limits and few dangerous side effects, and that by no stretch of the imagination imply environmental degradation.

Such confusion forces us to refine our understanding of economic growth. The definitions of economic and technological growth already introduced do not make specific allowance for environmental soundness or contribution to human welfare. All goods and services as they contribute to GNP and productivity are counted equally in dollar terms at market prices. It is assumed that environmental soundness and contribution to human welfare are either included in the price paid or are irrelevant. It is precisely this assumption which is now in question. GNP is roughly analogous to an overweight man. He may not want or need all the pounds he puts on.

Economic growth in which environmental soundness and contribution to human welfare are not requisites is for our purposes "undifferentiated growth." Undifferentiated growth is simply the increased "flow" of the economic system. Conversely, "differentiated" or "selective" growth is a form of growth in which environmental soundness and human welfare are taken into consideration.

Environmental soundness and contribution to human welfare are not very precise standards. They open up vast areas to subjective opinion and potential dispute. This is unavoidable in a debate that itself is highly subjective. To limit the range of subjectivity somewhat, we may say that environmentally sound growth is a type of growth in which the degree of pollution and of natural resource depletion does not: (1) exceed the long-range capacity of the globe to sustain the existing population at a margin above subsistence; (2) endanger health; and (3) destroy basic ecological support systems.

These criteria of environmental soundness do not mean the elimination of all pollution or of all resource consumption. Nevertheless, we encounter here the thorny problem of how to determine environmental soundness. Eventually, if there is to be environmentally sound economic growth, some global political body will have to determine acceptable limits to pollution and resource consumption on the basis of scientific, political, and ethical considerations. That such a body does not now exist leaves open the hard question of whether we will achieve this goal.

More problematic still is the criterion of human welfare. This concept speaks to the issue of the quality of life. No standard of quality acceptable to all exists. Yet, for the Christian there are clues, which can be derived from traditional notions of the Christian life, as to what this might generally mean. Within broad limits, for example, Christians will support forms of growth that relieve the sufferings caused by poverty, disease, and ignorance; they will criticize forms of growth that merely provide luxuries. They will also stand behind forms of growth that help to eliminate dehumanizing productive processes, do not require the creation of "needs" for their perpetuation, and are aesthetically pleasing.

Recent World Council of Churches discussions have suggested that human welfare has measurable and unmeasurable dimensions. For the measurable dimension there are maximum and minimum limits.

> Maximum limits can be determined by the quantity of resources available, the amounts of various resources which individuals and societies can use without waste, and the necessity to apply standards of distributive justice to all resources in relation to world-wide human need.
>
> Minimum limits depend on individual requirements. For example, daily protein and calorie intake necessary for the health and development of the body, the basic minimal requirements for clothing, housing, health care, and literacy can all be quantified and judged as to their quality. An adequate level should be provided beginning with those in greatest need.[3]

The unmeasurable dimension can be specified only in the most general terms. For World Council participants these general terms included:

1. Humanizing forms of community life.
2. Structures that permit the realization of a child's capacity.
3. Productive processes closely tied to local needs.
4. Opportunities for realizing creativity.
5. Participative decision-making.
6. Recognition and encouragement of diversity consistent with the well-being of the wider community.
7. Social structures which preserve tradition, yet increase awareness of the interdependence of all nations.

These and other examples we might offer are still not very precise. As with environmental soundness, concrete determinations of welfare can only be made through a political process. Even so, the problem is not basically one of precision. Criteria of welfare and environmental soundness can be developed. The problem is the creation of a consciousness that is open to the inclusion of these criteria and that sees them as primary, not secondary, considerations.

Beyond this we may note a few attempts to establish quality of life indices as alternatives to GNP. James Tobin and William Nordhaus have put together an instrument which they call the Measure of Economic Welfare (MEW).[4] Economist Charles Elliott cites a "development index" sponsored by the United Nations Research Institute for Social Development.[5] These and other similar indices exhibit considerable overlap and commonality. They suggest that there are several general criteria for measuring increasing human welfare besides the traditional economic ones. Chief among these are increases in education, health, housing, and diet.

Environmental soundness and contribution to human welfare are therefore the two main standards for sizing up the debate over growth. Additional standards will emerge, but it is important to keep these two always in mind. They add a measure of stability to the roller-coaster ride and will help us to assess the contrasting views of growth to which we now turn.

Chapter 2

CUSTODIANS AND CRITICS OF GROWTH

Material prosperity is no new concern of humankind. Until the time of the Renaissance, which is quite recent as history goes, scarcity and the struggle to cope with it were largely accepted as facts of life beyond rational control. Only in the late eighteenth century do we find the first significant attempts to articulate prosperity as a goal of human effort and to express rules governing economic expansion.

For Adam Smith (1723–1790) the wealth of a nation was the annual product of its labor. Its increase was governed, as if by an "invisible hand," through the free play of supply and demand that brought self-interest and the public interest into harmony. The responsibility of government was clearly secondary. Its role was to enforce contracts and to provide a few necessary public services. Growth was largely a result of individual initiative guided by the forces of competition.

Since Smith, economic and technological growth has increasingly become a goal of social policy in the industrialized nations. In contrast to Smith's theory, governments have increasingly attempted to take responsibility to stabilize and manage the growth rate. We are living in an age in which a vast majority of the electorate stresses both the importance of growth and the responsibility of government for its management. Indeed, during the past quarter century in the United States, growth has become the single most important goal of social policy.

The recent stress on growth stems from a number of well-documented developments. Advances in economic theory, triggered especially by the work of John Maynard Keynes, did much to provide planners with theoretical tools. The prosperity of the 1920's raised expectations of prosperity for all. The depression of the 1930's shattered confidence in laissez-faire attitudes and the automatic nature of the economic process. Together the theoretical advances, the raised expectations, and the shattered confidence contributed to a heightened consciousness of growth as an acceptable goal and to the need for governmental planners to stabilize and promote it.

Hand in hand with these developments came important changes in significant economic institutions of American society. During the first half of the twentieth century, American industry shifted from a structure characterized by small entrepreneurs to one in which a few large, technically oriented corporations dominated production. Corresponding to this shift was the rise of huge labor organizations with significant political and social power. Both industrial and labor leaders were receptive to governmental attempts to stabilize and promote growth.

World War II demonstrated that a large increase in government spending could raise employment levels and speed economic growth. In fact, it marked the turning point in America and other Western nations toward an explicit growth commitment. The Employment Act of 1946 recorded this commitment. It charged the government with responsibility for maintaining full employment, price-level stability, and, by implication, high rates of economic growth.

Perhaps even more important than these developments was the gradual acceptance by the vast majority of American citizens of the values and life-styles that were supportive of economic growth. This growth ideology, together with the changes in the economic structure, formed a powerful "thrust for growth" that reached a peak in the 1960's, a decade in which sustained growth and continuing abundance came to be accepted as the most important social policy goal.

Practically all Americans, at least in life-style or aspiration, are advocates of economic growth. The spokesmen for "all of us," however, tend to come largely from those groups who have benefited most from growth; they are the businessmen, politicians, lawyers, labor leaders, technologists, and economists who are the so-called "established" leaders of society.

Growth Becomes a Religion

The ideology of growth pervades American society as well as many other industrialized societies. This ideology has become virtually a religion. Individually and socially it shapes our value structure and determines our life-style. Unless this basic, underlying fact is understood, the difficulty of modifying our pattern of economic growth cannot be appreciated.

Advocates of growth build their case on this pervasive

ideology. Their position has several general characteristics that we will do well to keep clearly in mind. John F. Kennedy, in a speech to the graduating class of Yale University in 1962, highlighted several of these characteristics.

> The central domestic problems of our time . . . relate not to basic clashes of philosophy or ideology but to the ways and means of reaching common goals—to research for sophisticated solutions to complex and obstinate issues. . . .
>
> What is at stake in our economic decisions today is not some grand warfare of rival ideologies which will sweep the country with passion but the practical management of a modern economy. What we need are not labels and cliches but more basic discussion of the sophisticated and technical issues involved in keeping a great economic machinery moving ahead.
>
> The national interest lies in high employment and steady expansion of output, in stable prices, and a strong dollar. . . . To attain them we require not some automatic response but hard thought. . . .
>
> I am suggesting that the problems of fiscal and monetary policies in the Sixties . . . demand subtle challenges for which technical answers—not political answers—must be provided.[1]

In this excerpt are several of the familiar themes that punctuate the literature of those who stress the importance of economic growth. Common goals are assumed. Ways and means receive primary attention. Philosophies and ideologies are largely irrelevant. Basic research directed by practical managers seeking "objective" solutions is the only "rational" way through the complexities of modern society. Not passion, but planning, structures, and machinery are needed. The system must "move ahead," growth being equated to the national interest. And, of course, technical, not political, answers must be provided.

This by no means exhausts the emphases that characterize the pro-growth position. A summary list will help us to understand the growth-advocacy position and to appreciate its strengths and weaknesses:

1. An emphasis on structure, organization, form, method, and means.
2. A strong appreciation of science, technology, and empirical verification.
3. A need to eliminate risk and promote efficiency through planning and control of society and nature.
4. A view of nature as an instrument to be used for the welfare of persons.
5. An appreciation of a realistic, pragmatic, and "nonideological" style of decision-making.
6. A stress on specialized expertise.
7. A use of behavioral or functional social models in which a growing economic sector is assumed to be good and serves as a standard for measuring performance.
8. A short-run, progressively evolutionary view of the future.
9. A general sense of optimism based on a "faith" that social problems will be solved through timely applications of science and technology—the technological "fix."

Not every advocate of growth owns all these characteristics. There is, as one might expect, a good deal of diversity within the position. Some advocates come to the pro-growth position with considerable reservation about some of its aspects. Nevertheless, they have concluded that, on the whole, growth positively contributes to human welfare. At least among available alternatives it presents the best hope for the future.

By the mid-1960's, economic and technological growth had become an integral part of the *Zeitgeist.* Unprecedented prosperity abounded in those countries which had most fully exploited the fruits of science and technology. Insofar as this fantastic abundance was the goal of those who stressed economic growth, we may conclude that they were successful, at least for the moment.

Rumblings in the Wings

Nevertheless, at the precise time a minority of the world's people were enjoying the fruits of unprecedented material abundance on center stage, rumblings could be heard in the wings. Reaction to any strong thrust that involves change is never surprising. Change almost always benefits some at the expense of others. But who would argue with increased abundance?

Surprisingly, the challenge has come largely from those who have personally benefited from increased abundance. It did not arise from those who were hurt economically by growth or those whose gain was relatively small. If this were the case, we might have expected a significant outcry from the poor, whose economic position in the United States remains the same or has slightly declined during the past twenty-five years. Nor was the challenge so much a rejection of the goal of increased abundance and growth as it was the recognition of its deficiencies, the questioning of its long-range viability, and the challenging of technological authority.

As early as 1950, K. William Kapp pointed out the social costs of economic growth and the inadequacies of the Gross National Product as a measuring rod.[2] His voice, along with a few others, went unheeded. But in the 1960's the challenge gathered momentum. In 1962 Rachel Carson detailed certain side effects resulting from the extensive use of DDT to increase crop production.[3] Soon many ecologists joined her by pointing to other environmental abuses. As a consequence, by the late 1960's the ecology movement had come to life and mounted a well-publicized challenge to the prevailing growth ethos.

The developing challenge to growth did not rest solely on environmental grounds. Ezra J. Mishan, a British economist, expanded on the earlier judgments of Kapp in his widely read book, *The Costs of Economic Growth.*[4] In this volume Mishan moved beyond an ecological critique to raise questions about distribution of wealth, aesthetics, and significant values that were neglected in the obsession with materialistic goals.

Barry Commoner, one of the more articulate and moderate voices in the ecology movement, pointed telling criticism precisely at the new technologies that have been so important in post–World War II growth.[5] Many of these new technologies have been far heavier users of irreplaceable natural resources and more flagrant polluters of the environment than those which they displaced, according to Commoner.

Finally, an entirely different type of criticism came to the fore. This questioned the long-range viability of economic growth. Kenneth Boulding in his essays on "spaceship earth";[6] Herman Daly in his studies of the "stationary-state economy";[7] a team of computer specialists at M.I.T. headed by Dennis Meadows;[8] and a British group which has published a report called "A Blueprint for Survival" [9]—all in varying ways have concluded that a nongrowing, "sustainable society" will eventually be necessary.

These are only a few of the many voices raised in criticism of the prevailing stress on growth. Their challenge has roots in earlier movements and ideas. The ideas of Malthus, Ricardo, and Mill regarding limits and diminishing returns echo throughout the critiques.[10] Even the tradition of Thoreau and the return to rustic simplicity in nature finds expression.[11] The criticism of growth is by no means an entirely new phenomenon.

The critics are a diverse group. Many critical economists are actually advocates of growth who merely want more attention paid to its side effects or social costs. Some critics, in particular many ecologists and conservationists, think in much the same way as the advocates except that they see the natural environment, rather than the economy, as the whole which should be maximized. Others, the more liberal and militant, want to see the fruits of growth redistributed to the poor and the oppressed. Still others, members of the so-called "counterculture" and those alienated by the dominant culture, wish to substitute entirely different life-styles and ways of thinking. Finally, there are those who would call a halt to undifferentiated growth and institute a "sustainable society."

Can any coherence be found in such a diverse group? Contrary to appearances, the critical position is not one of total confusion. It is necessary first to separate those calling for a "sustainable society." They share a future-orientation and a concrete vision over against the other critics. For want of a better term, let us call them the "futurists," leaving the term "critic" to refer to those others who do not specifically take into account the long-range implications of growth.

The critics of growth also coalesce in opposition to the thrust for growth, though often at different points. Some object to the ethos, others to material side effects. In this opposition there are several recurring themes, most of which are also held by the futurists:

1. A distaste for the degree to which the social process is dominated by economic and technological considerations.
2. A stress on consciousness—that is, ideas, attitudes, values, life-styles, and experiences—over against structure.
3. An orientation toward the humanities—especially the arts, religion, ethics, aesthetics, and human relationships—as opposed to the sciences.
4. A focus on nature as the indispensable base of economic and technological growth.
5. A rejection of the view that nature is instrumental and hence exploitable.
6. A preference for conflict or voluntaristic models of society.
7. A short-range outlook.
8. A pessimistic view of the "technological fix," but often an optimistic view of the future given enough persons with changed attitudes.
9. An assumption of abundance.

Even a casual scrutiny of the critics reveals the almost total absence of representation from the poor and blue-collar classes of American society. Noting this same absence in Britain, Labour M.P. Anthony Crosland has attacked the critics as wealthy elitists.

> Their approach is hostile to growth in principle and indifferent to the needs of ordinary people. It has a manifest class bias, and reflects a set of middle- and upper-class value judgments. Its champions are often kindly and delicate people. But they are affluent and fundamentally, though of course not consciously, they want to kick the ladder down behind them.[12]

Whether or not Crosland's charge is correct, his comments introduce the often acrimonious conflict of ideologies that stands at the center of the debate.

In conclusion, we have three distinct parties in the growth debate: the advocates, the critics, and the futurists. None of these positions can be defined rigidly. The critical position in particular exhibits a great deal of diversity. Until recently the advocacy position has been unchallenged. It is the position in which most of us have been raised and which we have taken for granted. The critical position arose in the 1960's and is largely opposed to the advocacy position. It concentrates mainly on the question, Is growth desirable? The futurists take the long-range view and ask, Is continuous growth possible?

Growth as Means and End

In many important respects the positions of the critics and advocates resemble the positions taken during the cultural conflict of the 1960's. In its present form the growth debate became significant at the very height of that conflict. While it is clear that a relationship exists between that cultural clash and the growth debate, filling in the details is problematic.

Differences between the critics of growth and the dissidents of the 1960's are also obvious. Many of the critics, for example, do not fit within even the broadest limits of the so-called counterculture. Nor does the distinctive position of the futurists correspond very precisely to any movement of the period. Plainly also, the debate over growth has historical antecedents independent of the conflicts of the 1960's. Furthermore, that conflict was not exclusively concerned with economic growth.

It is also significant that the criticism of growth has increased at the very time the cultural conflict has largely been suppressed. The criticism of growth does not seem to be tied to the vagaries of alienated youth. It is more than a momentary ideological rebellion against established power, for at least one reason: the social costs of growth and the threat of depleted resources provide a firm and continuing basis for dissent. Concern for the environment, for the availability of resources, and for the higher visibility of nonmaterial values are not whims of the moment. They are deep-seated concerns with broad political appeal. There is therefore real danger in overplaying the coincidence of positions in the debate with the conflicting ideologies of the 1960's.

Suffice it to say that the growth debate has a relation to this conflict but is not historically or socially contained by it. The positions resemble each other but do not coincide. More tentatively, we may also conclude that the growth debate has carried forward several substantive aspects of the cultural conflict.

These general conclusions become more concrete when we ask a further question: what is at stake in the debate? The obvious answer is to reduce the dangerous side effects of growth and to determine the long-range capability of the earth to sustain undifferentiated economic growth. But this is by no means all or even the primary issue—though perhaps it should be. The primary issue in the debate is the imperialism of economic and technological considerations in determining values, ideas, life-styles, and social policy. Growth itself is not so much at issue as the ways we have allowed it to become both means and end.

It is growth in the driver's seat, growth as a sufficient end in itself that the critics and futurists primarily oppose. Their opposition represents a challenge to those who control the growth process and benefit most from it. What is also at stake is the dominant position of those whom we may call, for lack of a better term, the "custodians" of economic and technical power. Therefore, the growth debate is first of all a power struggle. The substantive questions of social costs and limits to growth are at present being contested largely on ideological grounds.

The custodians seem to be aware of this. Nowhere is this more evident than in their strong efforts to manipulate the media to enhance their own image. The advertisements of major oil companies, for example, would lead a casual observer to believe pollution is no problem, for they have everything under responsible control.

Or even more indicative of the power struggle are the visceral responses to such published reports as *The Limits to Growth* and *World Dynamics*, of the M.I.T. team. In general, neither the supporters of these reports nor their detractors speak about what of value may be learned from the project. Rather, most reviewers quickly jump to the heart of the matter, asserting their faith or lack of faith in the technological "fix." These responses, though sometimes based on reasoned and factual analysis, are too frequently ideological only. Clearly, something more personal is at stake than eliminating social costs or determining limits to growth.

When we say that the imperialism of economic and technological considerations and the dominance of the custodians are the most important issues, we are not suggesting that there are any altogether convincing accounts of this primacy and dominance. About the only thing we can say for sure is that many of the critics and futurists would like to see this imperialism reduced and the power of the custodians subordinated to wider social control and ethical considerations.

Criticism Takes Several Forms

Analyses of technological and economic primacy and the dominance of the custodians take several forms. A common position is that technology and economic growth have become autonomous forces dictating the shape, direction, and values of industrialized societies. The means have become both means and ends. In Marxist terms, the material substructure determines the ideational superstructure. In other words, the way we organize our society, especially the productive sector, in general determines how we think.

Perhaps the most extreme statement of this position is that of Jacques Ellul in his widely read book *The Technological Society*. In this volume Ellul concludes that we are entering the era of the "technological society" in which "technique" is no longer an instrument of humankind, but is in control. From this position, which tends to reify technology, there extends a continuum to less extreme variations on the theme of autonomous technology. At base they all point to the degree to which industrial societies have given "carte blanche" to technological innovation. Once a new technology is developed, a problem must be found for it to solve regardless of whether the problem is worth solving.

Another position, often based on Marxist theory, is that technology and economic growth are the instruments of power of a new elite—the custodians of technology. According to this view, we have a classic case of a dominant class co-opting subservient classes to pay for its play. Technology and growth are not only the instruments of domination; they also serve to legitimate and preserve the existence of the economic and technical elite.

This theory helps to explain two phenomena. First, the needs of this new elite are served by the paradox of technological radicalism and social conservatism, both of which characterize American society. Change that brings ever-increasing areas under the aegis of technical planning and instrumentation obviously enhances the position of this new elite. Likewise, the unchanged preservation of a social structure that encourages the expansion of technology—indeed, one of whose cardinal tenets is the unfettered autonomy of the businessman—leaves the new elite without effective challenge. Gibson Winter has stated this quite well:

> We are proposing, then, that the techno-culture cherishes innovation on its own terms. It accepts feedback but not authentic dialogue. By its nature such a society casts a network of controls over existence, programming the minds and futures of its youth. Consequently, the innovations

which it encourages only reinforce the system. Innovations in thought, politics and fundamental issues are taboo and will be suppressed with violence when they appear. So the vaunted innovation of the techno-culture occurs only within the narrow confines of its own programs. Challenges to the educational venture itself will simply not be tolerated. They bring into question the ground on which the techno-culture rests; that is, they question the premise that the system possesses the truth and loyalty to the system is equivalent to pursuit of truth.[13]

This theory also makes plausible the notion that economic growth functions as an ideology of technical power.[14] We have already noted that economic growth and the technological process are closely linked. Thus, if economic growth can be made to appear as a primary social goal, the interests that gain by increased technology and growth will be enhanced, in most cases in both relative and absolute terms. Hence the close connection John Kenneth Galbraith draws between growth and the technostructure in his book, *The New Industrial State.*

All this suggests that the custodians of technology determine their own objectives according to their own values and interests. There is no conspiracy, according to this theory. Technology is not autonomous. It is for the most part controlled by a particular class. It is used on projects that further the interests and increase the power of this class. What appears as autonomous technology and economic growth is merely the well-disguised success of the new elite in persuading society to accept the elite's goals as its own.

Victor Ferkiss introduces a slight variation on this theme when he disclaims the existence of any "new" elite that can be readily identified.

Indeed, the central danger facing humankind in the latter part of the twentieth century lies not in the autonomy of technology or in the triumph of technological values but in subordination of technology to the values of earlier historical eras and its exploitation by those who do not understand its implications and consequences but seek only their own selfish personal or group purposes. The new man with his vast powers is coming into existence as the servant of neoprimitive man. The sorcerer's powers are in the hands of a vain and foolish apprentice and disaster threatens.[15]

Finally, a more moderate position accounts for the primacy. It is the natural outgrowth of the unparalleled abundance and achievement of the economic process. Economic growth is legitimated by its fruits. If the fruits have become a bit sour in recent years, it is not so much the fault of technology and growth as it is a failure of the political process to achieve sufficient control. Technology is a human activity. It is the fundamental activity of man the toolmaker and cannot be wished away by speaking of its autonomy or its subservience to special interest. The problem is to provide political tools to manage the problems that unbridled technology and economic growth have created.

These three positions, each vulnerable to close criticism, are obviously at variance. Yet they hold in common the view that the economic process, an instrument of man the toolmaker, has not been subordinated to the domain of democratic politics and wider social values. Consequently, the process is perceived by critical observers as an external force out of control.

Our society, as many have pointed out, has traditionally handled the problem by giving completely free rein to technological change and opposing the most formidable

obstacles to social change. Since, however, technological
change in fact forces social changes upon us, this has had the
effect of abdicating all control over our social environment
to a kind of whimsical deity. . . . We never ask, do we want
this, is it worth it? . . . We simply say, "You can't stop
progress" and shuffle back inside.[16]

Each position no doubt contains a kernel of the truth.
But perhaps the most convincing brief account comes
from economist Robert L. Heilbroner, who claims that
the successes and failures of capitalism and socialism are
not so much a result of their differences as of their
common elements.

I identify these common elements as the forces and structures of scientific technology on which both systems depend
for their momentum. This suggestion would least seem to
need supporting argument in explaining the ability of both
systems to achieve economic growth. . . . All the processes
of industrial production that are the material end products
of scientific technology have one characteristic of overwhelming effect—their capability of enormously magnifying
human productivity by endowing men with literally superhu-
man abilities to control the physical and chemical attributes
of nature. Once an industrial system has been established
. . . it surely resembles a gigantic machine that asserts its
productive powers despite the sabotage of businessmen and
bureaucrats.

Industrial civilization achieves its economic success by
imposing common values on both its capitalist and socialist
variants. There is the value of the self-evident importance of
efficiency, with its tendency to subordinate the optimum
human scale of things to the optimum technical scale. There
is the value of the need to "tame" the environment. . . .
There is the priority of production itself. . . . All these
values manifest themselves throughout bourgeois and "so-

cialist" styles of life, both lived by the clock, organized by the factory or office, obsessed with material achievements, attuned to highly quantitative modes of thought. . . . It is a malady ultimately rooted in the "imperatives" of a common mode of production.[17]

Heilbroner's comments point to the subtle influence, even domination, of the economic process. To reify technology or to assert a grand conspiracy of a new elite is not accurate. There are truths in these assertions, but dominion is more subtle, though nonetheless powerful.

However, there are chinks in the armor of technical culture. While breaking down older cultural patterns, the economic process has not created a satisfactory new cultural synthesis. There are, as Heilbroner suggests, life-styles, values, and art forms consistent with a material base dominated by technology. But for too many people the resulting synthesis is too exclusive, its goals too limited, its vision too uninspiring. It is a low-order synthesis that neglects too many aspects of human life. It is unsatisfying, in spite of theological attempts to make it seem otherwise.[18] As long as dissatisfaction exists, alienation will be present and provide a continued basis for criticism.

In fact, the technologically dominated system we now have produces its own critics on a grand scale, often inadvertently. Not only through alienation, but perhaps more importantly through the schooling process criticism is nourished. The schooling process, which ironically is not crucial to the high-level functioning of the system, creates leisure, forces prolonged introspection in youth, and introduces the student to counter values. The university is probably the single most important preserve of counter values, and the system is vulnerable to the secondary effects of exposure to contrary ideas.

In addition, as Galbraith maintains in *The New Industrial State,* the men who run the large corporations are susceptible to social criticism. Their system of motivation, which depends on identification and adaptation, requires a consistency of goals between society and the large corporation.[19] Such consistency is now achieved in part by the societal acceptance of technology and economic growth as goals. But if the present legitimation of technology and growth is reduced, then the corporations are open to potential conflict.

Nevertheless, we should be on guard against simplistic statements about the impending and inevitable collapse of the existing synthesis in which economic and technological considerations play so central a role. The forces behind economic growth are strong and firmly entrenched. Opposition is relatively weak and unorganized. The ingredients of a new synthesis that could subordinate the economic process without destroying it are in the social mix but not yet in sufficient proportions to effect major change. The dough cannot rise until more of this new synthesis is sifted through the social fabric. Perhaps of greater importance is the need for yeast—that is, a certain combination of ideas, events, and material forces that will bring the old synthesis and its antithesis into greater conflict. That such a combination is possibly on the horizon is the contention of later chapters. For now, it is crucial to see that the existing synthesis is powerful and will not be overthrown by simplistic statements that it should be or that it is unfulfilling.

Thus the debate is in part a conflict of ideologies and values, in part a contest for power. While the critics and futurists seek to subordinate economic and technological considerations to other, nonmaterial values, the custodians of economic and technical power and most of the advocates of growth seek to maintain the *status quo* of constant technological change.

Actually, the conflict between the custodians and their critics is not new. It is well over a century old. Both the conflict of the 1960's and the criticism of growth can be seen in part as new phases of a much older battle against entrenched economic power.

Chapter 3

THE THRUST
FOR GROWTH

Words are frequently pregnant with implications. The terms we choose in discussing an issue not only reveal our own feelings about it but also possess a power to influence ideas and affect actions in others. Certain words constantly recur in descriptions of the growth process. Almost all have favorable connotations. Growth is equated with "progress." We are told that a "dynamic," "healthy," and "sound" economy is one that is "rapidly" or "vigorously" expanding. Third World nations are encouraged to "develop," that is, grow in accord with their "potential." Growth leads to an "enriched" life and a "rising standard of living." It increases "welfare" and human "well-being." Workers are exhorted to be "achievement motivated."

Correspondingly, opponents of growth and situations where there is no growth are described in negative terms. Opposition to "development" or "developers" "holds up progress," or "jeopardizes employment opportunities." "Idle" resources are those which the production process has not exploited. "Scarcity" needs to be "overcome."

An economy that is not growing is one that is "static," "stagnant," or in "depression." The opposite of a "bull" market—note the sexual imagery—is a "bear" market.

Consider further the connotations of words used to describe change. Economist Joseph Schumpeter characterized economic progress as a process of "creative destruction." [1] Ubiquitous advertisers urge us to be in the "van of fashion." Almost every product is "new" or "improved." Technological inputs are "advances," "breakthroughs," "innovations," or "improvements," sometimes given further potency by the adjective "creative." Finally, and most obviously, the word "good" is used to describe certain categories of output, as in the production of "goods" and services.

The use of such words and expressions is no mere coincidence, according to the critics. It epitomizes the degree to which economic growth has become an accepted part of the American way of life. Indeed, growth is more than just acceptable. It is something of a "fetish," say the critics. Take, for example, the way most standard economics texts rank countries by the size of their gross national product. Anyone even peripherally acquainted with competitive sports knows that the only place to be is at the top. Second place denotes a successful season, but only the top spot really matters. Such rankings remind one of Biblical and mythological characters whose success in battle is determined by whose god is stronger. By this criterion, America has a strong god indeed.

The religious analogy can be carried even further. The monthly release of economic statistics is accompanied by a ritual whose pattern is comparable to the rites that surrounded the pharaohs of ancient Egypt. Reported by the chief officials of the President's Council of Economic Advisers, the statistics are dissected in minutest detail and immediately passed on to lay devotees through the press and television. If the statistics are bad, immediate remedies are called for, usually in the form of various technical manipulations. The chief adviser is like the shaman who covers the fact that his prayers did not bring military victory by saying that the troops did not pray hard enough. Failure to produce the desired economic "benefits" calls for more vigorous policies to promote economic growth and technology.

Although this is something of a caricature, economic growth does possess many features of a religion, according to the critics. Economic progress is the hope of the system. Sin consists of ignorance, stagnation, and "nonrational" thinking. Salvation comes through economic and technological expansion. The blessing of God is a surfeit of material goods. In the words of physicist and Nobel Prize winner Dennis Gabor: "Unfortunately all our drive and optimism are bound up with continuous growth. 'Growth addiction' is the unwritten and unconfessed religion of our times. In industry and also for nations, growth has become synonymous with hope." [2]

Strictly speaking, obsessions with rank and religious analogies are not part of the growth process. Economic growth is a material process in which land, labor, capital, and science-based technology are brought together by organization to produce ever-increasing amounts of goods and services. Yet this material process does not stand alone. It is surrounded by ideas, values, life-styles, and propaganda, all of which serve to support and legitimate it. Together the material process and the surrounding ideological factors form a taken-for-granted synthesis that powerfully informs the thought and action of us all. This synthesis, which we call the "thrust for growth," now needs to be explored in some depth.

The Growth Record

First, let us review some statistics on economic growth and productivity. The growth record of the United States since 1910 shows an advance of about 3 percent per year except for the depression of the 1930's, the war years, and a slightly higher rate in the 1960's. Between 1929 and 1974 the overall annual growth rate (according to the *Economic Report of the President,* February 1975), was 3.1 percent. Broken down, the percentages run as follows: 1929–1945, 3.5 percent; 1945–1974, 2.9 percent; 1950–1960, 3.2 percent; 1960–1974, 3.8 percent.

From statistics issued by the U.S. Council of Economic Advisers, these percentages show a rise in GNP from $284.8 billion in 1950 to $1.397 trillion in 1974 in terms of current dollars. Translated into constant (1958) dollars, the rise is from $355.3 billion in 1950 to $821.1 billion in 1974.

The most accurate measure available for the effect of technology is productivity. According to statistics from the Department of Labor, Bureau of Labor Statistics, a rise of 3.2 percent per year was recorded for the period 1947–1969 and 3.3 percent for the period 1957–1969.

From figures compiled by the Department of Commerce, Bureau of the Census, we can get some idea of relative economic growth rates in various industrialized countries. The table of Average Annual Economic

Growth Rates shows three periods—1929–1967, 1950–1960, and 1960–1967—and the percentages given yield some significant comparisons.

Average Annual Economic Growth Rates

	1929–1967	*1950–1960*	*1960–1967*
United States			
Total	3.3%	3.2%	4.8%
Per Capita	2.0	1.5	3.3
Canada			
Total	3.8	4.0	5.3
Per Capita	1.9	1.3	3.3
France			
Total	2.1	4.6	5.1
Per Capita	1.6	3.7	3.8
West Germany			
Total	3.8	7.8	3.9
Per Capita	2.5	6.2	2.8
Italy			
Total	3.0	5.8	5.4
Per Capita	2.3	5.4	4.3
United Kingdom			
Total	2.3	2.7	3.0
Per Capita	1.7	2.3	2.3
Japan			
Total	4.6	9.3	10.2
Per Capita	(NA)	8.1	9.1

From these statistics it can be seen that the United States economy in recent years has grown at a slower annual rate than the economies of several other countries. Noteworthy also are the fantastic rates of Japan. The difference, of course, lies in the levels of GNP. The GNP of the United States, both total and per capita, is considerably higher than that of any other country.

Comparisons with the U.S.S.R. are tricky because of differences in economic systems and accounting methods. Nevertheless, economist W. Allen Wallis estimates that the Soviet economy has grown at an annual rate of 6 to 8 percent in recent years, though there is some recent evidence of a tapering off in this rate.[3]

The Anatomy of Growth

Economists have probed the phenomenon of economic growth sufficiently to understand in broad outline how it functions. Two basic sets of factors determine the output and growth of an economy. On the one hand there are the factors that determine aggregate demand: notably, consumption expenditures, residential investment, investment in plant and equipment, state and local government expenditures, inventories and exports.[4] On the other hand there are the factors which determine potential supply, the capacity of an economy to produce.

In any given period either the supply or the demand factor may limit the ability of the economy to grow. In periods of less than full employment, the demand factor has the more important effect. In such periods the economy is usually slack; excess supply characterizes several sectors at once. For the GNP to grow, aggregate demand must be stimulated to meet the supply. It is foolish to add to capacity until demand is strong enough to absorb it; otherwise producers confront idle plants and equipment.

In periods of full employment and full-capacity production, supply is the limiting factor. Unless producers increase the capacity of the economy, pressure on prices builds. In this situation the demand factor is less crucial. For the economy to grow, economic policy must stimulate the capacity to produce goods and services.

According to economist Robert M. Solow, while demand factors can be dominant sources of changes in national product in any given period, over the long range the supply or capacity factors must dominate.[5]

Five variables affect the growth of capacity: (1) the labor force, its size, age structure, participation rates, rates of unemployment, and average number of hours worked per week; (2) land; (3) investment in capital; (4) education; and (5) technology—research, invention, development of new ideas and organizations, and innovation resulting in increased productivity.

Economist Edward F. Denison has attempted to assess the relative importance of these variables in the growth process.[6] He estimates that from 1929 to 1957 the average annual growth rate of real national income in the United States was 2.93 percent. About one fourth of this rise was due to increased employment and hours worked, nearly one fourth to increased education, about one sixth to capital investment, and one third to increased technological efficiency. Land made no contribution in this period.

Note again the importance of technology in economic growth. Actually, its importance may be obscured in these percentages. If a broader definition of "technology" is used, one which would include the "advances in knowledge" incorporated in capital investment, education, and increased employment, then nearly 70 percent of the rise could be attributed to technological advance, according to Denison.[7] Our earlier assumption is confirmed. Technology is perhaps the single most important factor in economic growth. Likewise, because technological innovations require financing, economic growth is an equally important factor in the utilization of new technologies.

The effects of these factors are fairly obvious. Rapid economic growth promotes higher real wages, heftier profits, and rising material abundance. If this were not enough to recommend growth in a society that emphasizes work, profits, and consumption, there is an even more urgent need for it in advanced capitalist economies. Sustained and stable growth is essential to avoid unemployment and depression. This urgency arises out of the dynamics of investment first articulated by British economists Roy Harrod and Esvey Domar in the late 1930's.

In brief, a net rise in investment has two effects: it increases future supply by enlarging capacity. At the same time, it increases demand by consuming more goods and services in the process of enlarging capacity. If, however, expanded capacity is to be utilized, demand in the next period *must* also *increase.* If increased demand does not materialize, excess capacity induces investors to cut back on further plans to increase capacity. Such cutbacks reduce demand, and a downward spiral begins. In the words of economist Edward G. Shapiro:

> To justify today's net investment, tomorrow's must exceed today's in order to provide the additional aggregate demand needed to purchase that part of the enlarged potential output that is not purchased by consumers. In other words, as long as there is positive net investment, net investment must increase to prevent a decrease in net investment. The economy cannot stand still period after period with a

constant net investment; either it will move ahead (e.g., if autonomous consumption or government demand increases), or it will fall back.[8]

In blunt terms, our private market economy is on a treadmill. To avert mass unemployment, consumption and investment must continually increase. We cannot even stand still. Only growth averts "depression."

Neither the advocates nor the critics of growth dispute the logic of this state of affairs. The critics, however, see it as ecologically irrational. A treadmill that continually requires increasing the GNP will result, they say, in the depletion of resources and an escalating pollution crisis.

The Desire to Live Better

In areas of the world where per capita income is barely enough to sustain life and where existence is a day-to-day struggle, little consideration is given to abundance and high-level consumption. The all-important preoccupation is survival. If some surplus above mere sustenance is possible, the desire to rise above poverty seems universal. One might think that this level of material living would be enough for most people. But such is seldom the case. There seems to be a human impulse to keep on consuming material goods and services. Beyond the desire to live well there seems to be a desire to live better—to live better than before, and to live better than one's neighbor. Human wants are apparently insatiable.

Our understanding of the thrust for growth must include this fundamental phenomenon. Persons seem to want, even if they do not always enjoy, an ever-increasing supply of material goods. The progression of desire from the desire to live, to the desire to live better, is essential to the growth thrust. Explanations for this phenomenon abound. Some celebrate it. Others decry it as evidence of sin and depravity or as a tyrannical imposition of "group-think." But all explanations pale in the face of the phenomenon itself. So, with Adam Smith, it may be well to rest with this observation:

> It is in the progressive state, while the society is advancing to the further acquisition, rather than when it has acquired its full complement of riches, that the condition of the labouring poor, of the great body of the people, seems to be the happiest and the most comfortable. It is hard in the stationary, and miserable in the declining state. The progressive state is in reality the cheerful and hearty state to all the orders of society. The stationary is dull; the declining melancholy.[9]

This root of economic growth is understandable and in many respects desirable. As the growth advocates frequently attest, the process has in fact increased the quality of life in those countries that have experienced it. Citizens of those countries have better health care, they are better fed, better housed, and have better transportation. It has raised literally millions from the hopelessness of grinding poverty. It has made possible the pleasures of the arts, of travel, and of new friendships in cosmopolitan surroundings. Nor would many wish to exchange the benefits of growth for the conditions that existed prior to the Industrial Revolution. In short, growth is self-validating. Its fruits so far have outweighed its costs and have given powerful legitimation to its continuance.

Critics acknowledge these historical benefits. It is their opinion, however, that we have reached the point where the costs of additional growth now outweigh the benefits. In support of this view they point to pollution, depletion of resources, and various other side effects.

They also acknowledge the progressive nature of desire, but their response to this is more complex. They usually point to the fetish-like quality of the current desire for consumer goods, the injustice of unequal rates of progression throughout the world, and the ecological risks of giving in so easily to hedonism. Furthermore, some critics claim the current pursuit of goods and services is a classic example of whole societies relinquishing personal and social freedoms to economic determinism. Modern economies, especially capitalist economies, require high levels of consumption to maintain adequate demand. Consequently, in our "enslaved" state we have little choice but to consume more and more.

This claim of the critics stands at the center of the debate. Most advocates of growth would respond by saying that the great increases in consumption levels are a result of the free choices of individuals. The consumer is sovereign. He makes free decisions in the marketplace. The vast majority in our society are willing consumers. The economic system is merely an instrument serving the desires of this majority. While the system has imperfections and may exert some influence on the desires of individuals, it is basically sound and its reciprocating influence is really marginal.

Which is it? Have Americans molded their economic institutions or have economic institutions molded Americans? Or on a more theoretical level, do ideas shape social organizations, or do social organizations shape ideas? Whichever it is, even a casual observer cannot help but note the remarkable degree to which the ideas, values, and life-styles in most industrial countries support the economic process and its thrust for growth. The evidence seems to suggest *in this instance* that the economic process has been the dominant influence in shaping the way things are.

Two phenomena in particular support this conclusion: the shift in attitudes toward consumption and savings and the simultaneous retention of attitudes toward work and leisure as the American economy increased its capacity to produce more than just basic necessities. A closer look at these is in order.

Individuals have a choice between savings and consumption in deciding what to do with their income. Likewise in deciding what to do with their time they have a choice between work and leisure. In the early stages of economic expansion, savings and work were required for the system to grow. Investment and hard labor, not consumption and leisure, increased production capacity. Indeed, the impulses to consume and to rest had to be restricted. Corresponding to these needs of the system there were the two cardinal virtues, frugality and hard work; and the two vices, frivolous consumption and idleness.

These imperatives persisted into the twentieth century as the controlling element continued to be capacity, not demand. During the first third of the twentieth century, however, a change occurred. Capacity became sufficient to provide for basic needs. In fact, the economy became capable of providing much more. Investment and work had paid off. Yet, because of the ideology which held frugality and hard labor as virtues, demand beyond necessities was not sufficient to utilize capacity. This problem was a contributing factor to the great depression.

If the economy were to grow further, there was need for a change in attitudes. Individuals, and for that matter governments too, could no longer be frugal and hard working at the same time. If demand were to keep pace with capacity, individuals and governments had to combine higher levels of consumption with hard work.

As if on cue, there emerged in the first part of the twentieth century a new desire to consume more than the necessities of life. Alongside this shift from frugality to consumption, work attitudes remained nearly the same. "Work hard," "play hard"—precisely what the growing system needed. But which was it? Did shifting attitudes and desires cause the changes in the economy, or did management of demand through advertising and economic policy change attitudes and desires? More than likely both forces were at work, but in this instance the needs of the system seem to have played the dominant role.

The history of shifting attitudes toward consumption has been traced by economist Walter Weisskopf.[10] The original attitudes of frugality and hard work find their source in Calvinistic ascetisicm. There they were objectively anchored in a theistic system of considerable force. Frugality and hard work were thought to be the will of God for the elect. An early shift in this synthesis can be seen in the thought of Adam Smith. While holding values dear to the Calvinist, Smith sought to anchor them not in the will of God but in rational self-interest. A rational exploration of nature provided the necessary objective basis for frugality and hard work.

The Utilitarians, principally Bentham and Mill,

moved beyond Smith by introducing the pleasure principle. Pleasure, they thought, could be "objectively"
determined and roughly quantified. The things "objectively" pleasurable to them were precisely those activities
and values which undergirded the growing economic
system, in particular frugality and hard work.

Nevertheless, they had introduced a fateful element of
subjectivity by choosing pleasure as the ultimate guide
for action, and individual happiness as the ultimate
concern. To provide this subjectivism with some sort of
objective basis, the Utilitarians sought to quantify pleasure and pain using the notion of the greatest happiness
for the greatest number. This quantification was carried
one step further by neoclassical economists such as
Alfred Marshall. For Marshall, action was desirable if its
aim was to maximize monetary and consumptive gains.
Money and consumption became the measures of happiness.

The final step in this series of shifts was the *apparent*
elimination of value considerations altogether in the
twentieth century. Subjectivity, meaning the consumption of goods and services, won the day. What emerged,
claims Weisskopf, was the

> complete subjectivization and relativization of individual
> economic goals. No moral judgment, no objective value
> standard should be applied by the economist to individual
> preferences which determine the demand for goods. The
> realm of values is expelled from the realm of reason. Values
> are not only subjective, pluralistic, relative and different for
> different individuals; they are also irrational and not amena-
> ble to reasonable discussion. Value neutrality is pushed to
> the extreme and becomes complete value-emptiness. . . .
> Formal rationality empty of content and interpreted as the

maximization of subjective utility whatever it consists of, becomes the ultimate ideal.[11]

Thus advocates of growth assert that the consumer is sovereign and his goal is the active maximization of inner satisfaction. Yet there is no indication of what this satisfaction entails or how it can be achieved. It is as if individuals automatically know what makes for happiness. Actually, claim the critics of growth, values are not absent, only hidden. Happiness is given content by the dominant factors in the economic system.

Conscious deliberate maximization of satisfaction derives its pattern from technology and business and requires planning, budgeting, allocation in anticipation of future goals; then action according to plan, budget, allocation scheme, and finally reaping the reward of maximum satisfaction. The individual is mainly viewed as a consumer, and as such as a supporter of the production system. He has to show a certain stability in his behavior pattern; otherwise production could not catch up with demand. . . .

This model of behavior certainly underlies modern advertising which aims at seducing buyers into "binges" of spending. . . . Advertising psychology fits in precisely with the disintegration of economic rationality from a substantive idea to a content-empty subjectivistic scheme.[12]

The result is that maximization of inner satisfaction becomes the acquisition of money and of things money can buy. Satisfaction means maximum acquisition as measured quantitatively in terms of money. The void of "value freedom" is filled with values supportive of material consumption and ultimately of economic growth. The entire development, assert critics like Weisskopf, is merely part of the ideology of growth.[13]

In contrast to the shift in attitudes toward consumption, attitudes toward work have changed remarkably little. This is not to say present-day Americans hold to the Puritan work ethic in its classic form or necessarily that hard work is as prized as it once was. Rather, Americans generally have chosen to continue working a fairly constant number of hours per week rather than to transfer productivity into leisure.

By some accounts this is a strange turn of events. One of the promised benefits of economic growth has been increased leisure. Indeed, for a time the number of hours worked on the average showed a steady decrease. But since World War II, this decrease has been arrested. In addition, the percentage of the population at work has increased from 56 percent in 1940 to 60 percent in 1973.[14]

Why has work not been traded for leisure? In 1959 the Joint Economic Committee of the United States Congress observed:

> The large and increasing amount of multiple-job holding, particularly in industries with short workweeks, as well as the rising participation of married women in the labor force suggests that where families have a choice between leisure and more money income, many of them choose more income.[15]

Persons do not elect leisure because they prefer consumption. The alternatives to most of us are not work and leisure, but consumption and leisure. To consume we must work both because consumer goods must first be produced and because a job is the only satisfactory means to adequate income for consumption.

Hence on two counts the continuing preference for work over leisure contributes to a growing economy. It makes the production of goods easier and the consumption of goods possible. Furthermore, this preference for work is encouraged both by the current emphasis on full-employment and a still vital work ethos. With Walter Weisskopf we can observe:

> employment and a traditional kind of job also perform a psychological function. They give meaning to life which, in Western society, is based on one's function in the economy. Work in a traditional job is considered as the only legitimate way of life. It is not only the basis of external status but also of self-respect. This invests the goal of full employment with a socio-psychological importance which transcends the purely economic arguments of incentives and purchasing power.[16]

What we have then, according to the critics, is a rather neat circular system with its own momentum and supporting ideology. While high-level consumption fills the demand needs of a growing economy, high-level productiveness fills the supply needs. What is produced must be consumed and what is consumed must be produced. In the words of critic Philip Slater: "What all our complex language about money, markets and profits tends to mask is the fact that ultimately, when the whole circuitous process has run its course, we are producing for our own consumption." [17]

Many critics see this circularity as highly manipulative. So-called "consumer sovereignty" is actually producer sovereignty and consumer slavery. It covers over the degree to which demand is manipulated. Other critics claim current consumption patterns are superficial. Real human needs are left unmet as pseudo needs are created and exploited. Still other critics point to the injustice of 6 percent of the world's people, the Americans, consuming approximately 40 percent of the world's resources. Finally, the futurists predict adverse consequences will result from such a profligate use of resources.

Critics seldom attack work itself. Rather, the criticism is directed at the work ethos, in particular its sometimes excessive and obsessive quality. Critics also point to the alienation involved in many forms of work, for instance, its repetition, boredom, and uncreative nature. Finally, they claim the continuing preference for work over leisure is socially created. It represents an abdication of human freedom to the economic system.

The advocates of growth make little effort to apologize for the circularity. Why "knock" a good thing? When occasionally they do respond, it is usually to point out how much of the criticism is caricature; how it obscures the real benefits of growth; how difficult it is to organize and maintain an economic system; and how many of the critics are elitists. As for manipulation, no one is forced to consume or work.

Another element in this circular process is advertising. We should avoid attributing too much influence to advertising, but that it is one of the forms of demand manipulation can hardly be denied. The critics claim that advertising is one of the primary means used in our society to channel subjective impulses toward the objectives of production and consumption.

For critic Jacques Ellul, the primary purpose of advertising "is the creation of a certain way of life." [18] It is not so important that advertising convince the consumer about a given product as it is to persuade him to accept a certain style of life. The product for sale must be made to seem indispensable to some ideal, and for Ellul this ideal is the technical way of life. Once the consumer accepts this way of life, the mission of advertising shifts to specific needs, which in turn create pressures to buy selected products. The creation of needs, however, presupposes and depends on the acceptance of the ideal.

John Kenneth Galbraith claims that advertising is rooted in the need of large corporations to manage demand.

> The need to control consumer behavior is a requirement of planning. Planning, in turn, is made necessary by extensive use of advanced technology and capital and by the related scale and complexity of organization. These produce goods efficiently; the result is a very large volume of production.[19]

This large volume must be disposed of if the producer is to survive. The producer, following instincts of survival, in turn tries to ensure that such disposal takes place. Advertising, by influencing the distribution and quantity of demand, increases the flow of revenue to those who advertise. In so doing, it allows the firm to have some measure of control over the revenue it receives. "The general effect of sales effort . . . is to shift the locus of decision in the purchase of goods from the consumer where it is beyond control to the firm where it is subject to control." [20]

In sum, according to critics of economic growth, advertising serves to channel impulses toward consumption and production by creating and reinforcing a way of life. This way of life includes competition, the manufactured illusion of scarcity, and the fulfillment of needs through the purchase of goods and services. The purpose of this channeling of impulses is to maintain the high-level demand necessary for a growing economy, to legitimate the primary producers of growth, to control the demand for products, and to promote work incentives. An unintended product, however, is a widespread sense of alienation. Unimportant needs become felt needs, the possibility of satisfaction is eliminated, and women become the object of sexual exploitation. Ultimately, there is a loss of freedom. Choices are artificially created. Avenues that might lead to freedom for millions through the elimination of poverty are blocked by pseudo priorities.

Advertising is not without supporters. Beyond the obvious argument that advertising promotes growth and full employment, advocate Yale Brozen points to its educative functions.[21] It informs the consumer as to use, desirability, price, and quality of a given product and thereby better equips him to make wise selections. Furthermore, claims Brozen, advertising promotes competition, lowers prices in certain instances, and supports many forms of public communication.

Perhaps the most convincing argument is that advertising and consumer buying is offering all people what before only a few had. Through advertising and mass consumption, goods and services are being more widely disseminated. What the critics are really concerned about, according to the advocates, is not exploitation, economic determinism, and alienation, but the democratization of American life.

No resolution of the many conflicts between the critics and advocates appears imminent. Simply to clarify the issues is a considerable advance. In areas such as this where facts are so hard to come by and where opinions are as numerous as the debaters, agreement is simply impossible. We can, however, offer a few observations that will stand no matter what view is taken regarding economic determinism, or the desirability of present life-styles, or the pros and cons of advertising: (1) the debate is highly ideological; (2) the circle of work-advertising-consumption is a critical factor in the thrust for growth; (3) ethical issues—for example, freedom and coercion (manipulation), the ideology and elitism of the debaters, the distribution of income and wealth, and preeminently the desirability of growth—are central to the developing debate.

The World View of Science and Technology

Individuals and groups invariably give order and meaning to experience. The term "world view" refers to the conceptions and schemes that are produced. World views are frames of reference. They come in varying degrees of coherence and articulation. Frequently they seem to have a life of their own. They are accepted as "The Truth," or they become alien objects that act back on us as if they were divine, not human, products. A pluralism of world views has characterized the twentieth century both nationally and internationally. Despite this pluralism, there have been common elements, the most important being a high valuation of science, technology, and economic growth. Indeed, one might even broaden this and refer to this common valuation as the world view of science and technology. It prevails especially in the industrialized nations.

The historical process by which this world view largely supplanted religious and other world views is referred to as secularization. This process is complex and not entirely understood even today. Yet we can say that with the development of science, the marriage of science and technology, and the wide acceptance of positivistic philosophy, there occurred a gradual transformation in the way that persons in the industrialized countries viewed reality. While traditional world views have not been entirely supplanted, this world view of science and technology has become dominant.

It is seen by those who hold it not as a historically conditioned, social product, but as the truth. Because it has been imparted to us in the process of socialization, most of us take its valuations and ideas for granted. Some holders of this world view have even declared the "end of ideology." In place of the unprovable, unverifiable, and subjective elements in other world views, they want us to subscribe to the "objectivity" of positivism and the scientific method. They fail to see that they are only substituting one world view for another. This blindness, however, does not alter the remarkable conquest of minds and attitudes that has accompanied the world view of science and technology.

Certainly one of the primary reasons for this conquest was the fruit it has borne. The discoveries of science, the improvement in material living standards, and increasing affluence made a deep impression on human minds. The proof was in the pudding.

Several features characterize this world view. The assumptions of the advocates of growth outlined in our second chapter are representative. To cite another example, scientist Eugene Schwartz enumerates twelve axioms of the science-technology world view:

1. Man is not naturally depraved.
2. The "good" life on earth is not only definable but attainable.

3. Reason is the supreme tool of man.

4. Knowledge will free man from ignorance, superstition, and social ills.

5. The universe is orderly.

6. This order can be discovered by man and expressed in mathematical quantities and relations.

7. Although there may be many ways of perceiving nature—e.g., art, poetry, music, etc.—only science can achieve "truth" that will enable man to master nature.

8. Observation and experimentation are the only valid means of discovering nature's order.

9. Observed "facts" are independent of the observer.

10. Secondary qualities are not measurable and hence not real.

11. All things on earth are for use by man.

12. Science is neutral, value-free, and independent of morality and ethics.[22]

This world view legitimates the economic process. It makes economic growth seem natural and desirable, and its continuation axiomatic. In Marxist terms it is an ideal superstructure built on the substructure of existing economic relationships. Its immediate beneficiaries are those who control these relationships.

To a remarkable degree the debate over growth is a debate between conflicting world views. To identify the ideological overtones of the debate is crucial to its understanding. The contrasting ideas, values, and life styles of some critics are more a result of dissatisfaction with this world view than with growth itself.

Two aspects of this world view call for further scrutiny, both because they are in their own right factors in the thrust for growth and because they raise important ethical and theological issues. In Schwartz's list of axioms the quantification tendency in axiom 6 and the utilitarian view of nature implied in axiom 11 point to these aspects. Nature and, to a lesser degree, persons are instruments to be used for the welfare of humankind (or, according to the critics, for the perpetuation of existing economic relationships).

This instrumental view of nature stands in stark contrast to many non-Western views in which nature is sacred. Indeed, it stands in contrast to certain strands in Judaism and Christianity in which nature is an end and not a means. Why this view of nature arose in the Christian West is a matter of much recent speculation. Medieval historian Lynn White, Jr., attributes it to the "dominion" texts in The Book of Genesis and Christian natural theology. Critics of White cite other factors. Whichever causative version we accept, the view itself remains.[23] Even more, it becomes an issue in the debate.

According to the critics, the economic and technological process in its present form dangerously exploits nature through depletion and pollution. The instrumental view of nature has made exploitation easier by removing psychological and ethical restraints that might otherwise have been present if nature were seen as an end or a good in itself. Further, the instrumental view has been an important source of the continuing blindness of us all toward environmental degradation.

Hand in hand, claim the critics, an instrumental view of persons has developed. This view of persons is not, of course, an explicit axiom of the world view. No one advocates turning people into "tools." Nevertheless, this is implied, particularly in its tendency to see persons in terms of numbers. The world view of science and technology is inherently insensitive to persons and nature. Labor and land, for example, are "factors" and "costs" of production. Human beings consequently are subjected more easily to dehumanizing advertisement and alienating forms of work and consumption. In short, the exploitation of persons and nature, according to the critics, is both consequence and cause of the world view. The world view desensitizes us, and the resulting exploitation contributes to the thrust for growth, thereby perpetuating the world view.

The Idea of Progress

Closely related to the world view of science and technology is the idea of progress. The word "progress," usually defined as improvement or advance toward a higher state, is heavily laden with value connotations. It is frequently linked to economic growth, even to the degree that the words "progress" and "growth" are used interchangeably.

Economist Paul W. McCracken opens an essay whose title, "The Mainsprings of Economic Progress," is itself revealing, with these comments on the growth of the gross national product:

> What explains this long-sustained record of economic advance? The average American, not much given to reflection, would probably be surprised only that the question would be asked. Economic progress, we seem to assume, must be something like death and taxes—it just automatically comes with the passing of the years.[24]

Or consider how economist W. Allen Wallis equates growth and progress:

> Here is the real "nub" of the present growth debate: How to grow? What public policies will best promote economic

expansion in a free society? Where lie the pathways to progress? How we answer these questions will determine how well our economy in the Sixties converts its potentialities into realities.[25]

These are not just isolated examples. In fact, the equation of progress and economic growth is pervasive in economic literature. At first glance this is rather surprising, given the general retreat from cultural optimism following World War I. Especially in politics and religion the progressive outlook of the nineteenth century has dramatically changed. But it has not been so in science, technology, and economics. The idea of progress has hung on in a form that closely resembles the nineteenth-century outlook, and only recently has the voice of the critics been raised against it.

The equation of growth with progress builds upon a metaphor deeply imbedded in the Western mind. According to sociologist Robert A. Nisbet, whose study of growth is a classic in the history of ideas: "Of all metaphors in Western thought on mankind and culture, the oldest, most powerful and encompassing is the metaphor of growth." [26] Even so, the metaphor of growth cannot be directly applied to economic and technological expansion. Growth draws into the analogy the entire life cycle of an organism—birth, development, decay, and death. For this metaphor to be of legitimating service, somehow the last two stages, decay and death, must be ignored. Here the idea of progress comes into play. It modifies the more encompassing idea by emphasizing only birth and development. Therefore, the psychically potent metaphor of growth, shorn of its negative second half, is appropriated for economic and technological expansion. Thus, such expansion is seen as natural to and immanent in evolving societies. It develops continually through ever more mature stages. It has direction and purpose in serving the well-being of people, though indeed the content of that well-being is not precisely articulated. It is, in a few words, like the normal maturation of a child into adulthood.

As for this marriage of progress to economic and technological growth, critic Eugene Schwartz thinks the "dice are loaded."

> At first glance it appears that most problems that have been dealt with in the past three hundred years have been amenable to technological solution. Yet the success of science and technology was predetermined, in a sense, by selecting for solution only those problems that could be solved. Unsolvable problems were not accepted as real problems. Failures did not receive public notice. With the players themselves, scientists and technologists, establishing the rules and calling the score, success was inevitable—especially when the players were also allowed to define success.[27]

We will want to ask whether the growth debate signals the beginning of the end for the marriage of economic and technological expansion to the ideas of progress and growth. If it does, are industrial societies about to embark on a period of cultural pessimism analogous to decay and death in an organism's life cycle? Recognizing that the cyclical view of history is not the Christian view may prompt a prematurely negative answer. But such a response should be guarded, since the contrasting Christian view of history merely contests the validity of the analogy. Indeed, Christianity has a substitute notion for decay and death. It is the judgment of God, which both sides in the debate would do well to consider.

The Technostructure

Theologian André Dumas has called growth "an ideology which conserves technical power." [28] Dumas does not elaborate on this statement, but it points to a recurring theme among critics of growth. In Marxist terms, the nonmaterial factors in the thrust for growth are all part of an elaborate ideology that benefits the planners and executives of large corporations. Stated more modestly, the planners and corporate executives have found in the growth ethos a powerful tool to preserve and increase their own autonomy and power. Having found it, they have also added to it and given it direction.

John Kenneth Galbraith in his book *The New Industrial State* offers a persuasive account of this view. A new group, he says, has risen to dominance because of the imperatives of technology. Modern technology requires large capital investment and complex organizational structures. These in turn necessitate detailed planning of every step in the production process from investment to sales. As a result, the factor of production in scarcest supply is the technical expertise needed to organize and run this complex machinery. Such expertise, quite beyond the capacity of any one person, requires group decision-making. To those who perform the decision-making function in the two thousand or so large corporations that control 80 percent of the total assets used in manufacturing,[29] Galbraith has given the title "the technostructure." [30] For the most part this group consists of those who bring specialized knowledge to the various aspects of corporate decision-making.

As the technostructure has gained power and influence, the goals of the large corporations have correspondingly shifted away from making maximum profits. This is largely because the technostructure provides talent and not capital.[31] As long as profits are sufficient to keep shareholders from interfering and to eliminate the need for recourse to the capital funds market to finance investment, there is no particular incentive to maximize profits. The decision-making group, once minimum profits are assured, can turn to essentials, in particular to the preservation and increase of its own autonomy and interests. But autonomy and self-interest are seldom the stated goals of any group. Usually they are disguised by appeals to the general welfare or other legitimating devices.

Such is the case with the technostructure. Here Galbraith links the technostructure to the thrust for growth by entering the complex area of motivation theory. Members of the technostructure are motivated not so much by money as by the need to identify with a socially useful organization or to feel that the organization is potentially adaptable to their own social goals.[32]

This being so, the corporations need to pursue what appear to be socially useful ends in order to maintain the allegiance of their technostructures.[33] This leads to an important corollary:

> The relationship between society at large and an organization must be consistent with the relation of the organization to the individual. There must be consistency in the goals of the society, the organization and the individual. And there must be consistency in the motives which induce organizations and individuals to pursue these goals.[34]

Since the technostructure controls the large corporations,

the goals of the corporations will be those of the members of the technostructure and at the same time those of the society. If society places great emphasis on economic growth or technological virtuosity, then it may be expected that the technostructure will too.

The crucial question then becomes: Who in fact sets the goals of society? Does society adapt the technostructure to its values or is it the other way around? Galbraith seems initially to opt for the primacy of the technostructure in this process.

> What counts here is what is believed. These social goals, though in fact derived from the goals of the technostructure, are believed to have original social purpose. Accordingly, members of the corporation in general, and of the technostructure in particular, are able to identify themselves with the corporation on the assumption that it is serving social goals when, in fact, it is serving their own.[35]

The harmony of corporate and social goals is a by-product of corporate planning. It reflects, in Galbraith's terms, "the triumph of unexamined but constantly reiterated assumption over exact thought."

> The belief that increased production is a worthy social goal is very nearly absolute. It is imposed by assumption, and this assumption the ordinary individual encounters, in the ordinary course of business, a thousand times a year. Things are better because production is up. There is exceptional improvement because it is up more than ever before. That social progress is identical with a rising standard of living has the aspect of a faith.[36]

Actually, the primary goals of the technostructure are survival and autonomy. These goals are fairly easily reached by maintaining a minimum level of earnings that satisfies the stockholders and eliminates the need to go into the money markets. But according to Galbraith, nothing more insures the maintenance of these earnings, and consequently the survival and autonomy of the technostructure, than corporate growth. By advocating the growth of the economy, the technostructure promotes the growth of the firm and ultimately its own autonomy and power. At the same time it is seen as making a real contribution to society.

Returning to the question of whether society or the technostructure is the adapting agency, Galbraith finally asserts a "two-way influence." [37] Yet it is clear from what he has said that it is no mere coincidence that growth as a goal has received its greatest emphasis at the same time that the technostructure became a dominating influence in the industrial sector. This leaves us with a "soft" judgment: the technostructure is but one among many factors in the thrust, though indeed one that lends some measure of coherence to the whole.

The technostructure thesis gives rise to new criticisms of the growth process. Galbraith himself is among the critics of undifferentiated growth. The primary question Galbraith raises is the question of the degree to which the growth process is a tool of societal manipulation in the hands of a new elite. This raises serious ethical questions about freedom and the distribution of power. More fundamental still is the question, How desirable is a process that benefits some far more than others at the same time that it is propagandized as a social good for all? Indeed, growth as an ideology may be covering over some of the most serious social problems of the twentieth century.

Worthy of particular note are the military and high-

way industrial complexes. To what degree have the
interests of the technostructure and the ideology that
supports them led to vast and wasteful military expenditures and the overallocation of resources to roads? The
significance of this question is seen when we realize that
of the total research and development done by American
industry (about 70 percent of the nation's total), over 60
percent is financed by the Department of Defense and
NASA.[38]

Two Political Factors

In conclusion, two significant political factors in the
thrust for growth require brief mention. The first is
nationalism and defense. Nationalism was an early
contributor to the growth process. As a political movement it helped to provide the unified base upon which
growth depends. More important, however, nationalism
has been a continuing source of the thrust since growing
productive capacity is an essential element in the competition between nations. A high rate of economic growth
serves nationalism in several ways. It confers prestige. It
provides an increasing capacity to produce the instruments of war. And it augments economic power in the
competition for new markets.

By far the most significant of these is the second.
Economic growth and defense are mutually reinforcing
objectives. Indeed, one of the primary arguments for
growth is that it will increase America's ability to defend
herself. Though made more complex by nuclear weapons, this argument remains convincing to many.

The second political factor is the short-range orientation and responsive nature of the systems of government

found in most industrial countries. Periods of time vary among countries, but the intervals between elections are generally short. Politicians operating under the gun of the next election necessarily orient their responses to immediate economic needs and interests, many of which are satisfied by growth. Quite simply, our livelihoods depend on jobs, and full employment within our present structures presupposes economic growth. Add to this the funding of political campaigns, largely by businessmen and organized labor, and we leave the politician seeking reelection with no choice but at least to pay lip service to growth. No government can hope to survive the next election without employing the resources of fiscal and monetary policy to stimulate growth.

In summary, then, we may say that the thrust for growth is a complex amalgam of historical, ideological, economic, social, and material factors. The most important point to observe is the strength of this thrust. While it is not all-encompassing, the thrust is a powerful synthesis of ideal and material factors that will not easily be deflected.

Within this synthesis material factors seem to dominate the ideal factors. There is a fairly high consistency between the needs of the developing economic-technological process and the content given to commonly held values and beliefs. This consistency seems to owe much more to the developing process than it does to independent, ideological considerations.

Criticisms of the alienating and manipulative aspects of this synthesis abound. There is even some movement away from participation in the economic process. Yet we should be reserved in predicting the collapse of the process and wary of underestimating its staying process.

The challenge so far mounted is primarily ideological. It has been of small consequence to the material side of the synthesis. With the possible exception of the limits-to-growth criticism of the futurists, there appears to be little on the immediate horizon to cause major alterations in the synthesis. It is of course possible that the various criticisms signal the beginning of major change in the thrust for growth, but at present this is far from obvious.

Chapter 4

THE COSTS AND BENEFITS OF GROWTH

At the beginning of the great depression in 1930, economist John Maynard Keynes conjectured that the "economic problem" will be solved within a hundred years. A point will be reached, he suggested, when economic needs will be satisfied and we can devote our energies to noneconomic goals. From the avarice and greed of present economic pursuits, we will return to principles of religion and "traditional virtue." Ends will be valued above means, the good above the useful, and those capable of taking direct enjoyment in things will once again be honored. In a moment of greater realism Keynes concluded:

> But beware! The time for this is not yet. For at least another hundred years we must pretend to ourselves and to everyone that fair is foul and foul is fair; for foul is useful and fair is not. Avarice and usury and precaution must be our gods for a little longer still. For only they can lead us out of the tunnel of economic necessity into daylight.[1]

In Keynes's mind economic growth is desirable because it can release us from the determinism of economic necessity. Its purpose is to bring into being a society where humans can afford to let nonmaterial considerations rule their conduct. Now, nearly midway in Keynes's time perspective, the debate over growth is testing his hopes and predictions. Is growth with its many side effects leading toward the vague utopia he hoped for? Are we willing to put up with the undesirable aspects of a process that offered in Keynes's vision such grand rewards in spite of the economic depression during which the vision was drawn? In other words, is undifferentiated economic expansion desirable?

This preeminently ethical question stands at the center of the debate. Some may wonder why we consider whether growth is desirable before we ask whether it is possible. After all, doesn't the question become academic if in twenty years radically limiting governors will be necessary?

The reply to this is quite simple. Only recently has the debate included the question of long-range limits; the bulk of attention remains on short-range environmental problems. More significantly, the eventual necessity of the equilibrium economy proposed by the futurists is not yet altogether clear. Their work, based on partial evidence and the theoretical logic of exponential growth within fixed limits, has still to be thoroughly scrutinized. Since the possibility of indeterminate growth is still an open question, it is premature to declare the question of desirability academic. And most important, it is crucial to recognize that a fairly strong case can be made for undifferentiated growth in the absence of long-range limiting factors. Unless this is understood, we will be unprepared to face the difficulty of slowing, much less stopping, the thrust for growth. We must anticipate the possibility of an impending clash between the "good" of undifferentiated growth and the "necessity" of a no-growth or differentiated growth economy.

Thus the main question at issue in the next three chapters is the desirability of undifferentiated growth in the absence of conclusive evidence as to its viability. The word "desirability" used in this context has limitations. The critics and the advocates clearly differ both in what they find desirable and in the grounds for their judgments. Each group is attempting to make a rational case for its particular view in an effort to influence the future course of social policy. To give order to the conflicting assessments of desirability, we shall use the two criteria—environmental soundness and contribution to human welfare—outlined at the end of the first chapter.

Arguments for Growth

Advocates of economic growth say that, *on balance,* growth is desirable. This does not mean they favor high levels of pollution or like to see resources wasted. Rather, they judge the benefits of growth to outweigh the costs and are relatively optimistic about overcoming the serious problems associated with growth. With Keynes, they feel that the growth process will continue to eliminate the determinism of economic necessity.

The arguments for growth make a good case in theory and are powerful in practice. Perhaps the most appealing of them is the "extra-product" argument. Each year the growth process adds to the economy material resources that can be allocated as the society sees fit. This addition of material resources, or extra-product, permits more to be done, more problems to be solved. Measured against the criterion of human welfare, this argument is particularly persuasive when the possibilities of ever-improved social benefits are pointed out. Higher quality health care for the poor, mass transportation, urban renewal, and even environmental protection are made increasingly feasible through the extra-product, without necessarily reducing personal consumption. Indeed, some advocates of growth contend that continued growth is the *sine qua non* of eliminating poverty, largely for political reasons. Western societies are not prepared to redistribute income and wealth, these advocates claim, which leaves only the growth process as a means of removing material want.

A closely related argument contends that economic and technological growth is necessary to maintain, not to mention increase, the present "standard of living." With a growing population, simple arithmetic points to the necessity of growth in order to maintain real GNP per capita at a constant level. Growth is also necessary to avert the downward cycle of demand and investment discussed in the preceding chapter. But theory and arithmetic aside, not many of us would voluntarily elect a lower "standard of living." And this is true whether or not the "standard of living" concept is a useful one, given its vagueness, its material bias, and its use for ideological purposes, as well as the absurdly high level of the standard in some cases.

There is also the obvious need to keep employment levels high. Each year the number of persons holding jobs or seeking employment increases. Furthermore, the primary and only adequate source of income in the United States (unless, of course, one is wealthy) is a job. These two elemental facts are the basis of the demand for full employment. To achieve full employment, given present structures, growth is a necessity. Critics may find the range of choice between growth and unemployment unacceptably narrow; but in the short run, unemployment or growth is the choice.

Still another argument for growth is that it helps to prevent social strife, or at least is thought to do so. Advocates claim economic expansion not only keeps employment levels high and thus gives the employed a stake in continuing prosperity, it also makes possible the steady stream of goods and services that people need and want. Thus, as long as everyone is receiving a bigger piece of pie, there seems to be a tendency in the short run to be satisfied. This is so even if the piece the poor get is a constant or decreasing share of the total. Economic growth makes the pie bigger and everyone is happy, or so the thinking goes.

Growth does not eliminate all social strife, as even a quick look at the 1960's makes amply clear. Social strife is far too complex a phenomenon to have a single cause. Nevertheless, as the 1930's demonstrate, economic depression is a potential source of strife. During a depression the inequalities of income and wealth stand out starkly as each person seeks to mitigate his or her own loss.

Under a rather loose rubric of foreign policy, three additional arguments are offered in favor of growth. First, advocates claim that growth makes it easier for richer nations to render economic assistance to poorer nations, both through specific programs and increased trade. This is a potent argument ethically, and it remains so even if the realities of international economic assistance are meager in comparison to the potential.

The second of the foreign policy arguments is ethically less compelling but shows a realistic understanding of international relations. Growth, claim some advocates, makes available an ever-greater amount of material goods with which to pursue international objectives and to provide for defense needs. The truth of this claim can be seen by comparing United States involvement in Vietnam on the one hand and World War II on the other. In the Vietnam war relatively few restraints on consumption were necessary in comparison to the "total" effort of World War II, which was fought on a smaller economic base.

Ethically there are grave problems with militarism in this argument. Nevertheless, it has a powerful appeal. Each nation has legitimate defense needs, and the realities of international politics involve competition, one base of which is economic potential. The idea that these realities will change quickly is an illusion.

Third, there is the argument that economic growth has a "demonstration effect." In the case of the United States, it asserts that a strong, growing economy is necessary to make the capitalistic system more attractive than its chief rival, communism. This "demonstration effect" is important both for morale at home and in the competition for the uncommitted.

Ethically this argument is even more problematic than the preceding one. It has an imperialistic and nationalistic bias. It is a product of a cold war ideology that has helped to perpetuate vast military establishments at incredible expense. It presupposes an appeal to pride, encourages international divisions, and suggests that the aim of foreign policy is to control people's minds. Yet, despite its ethical difficulties, such an argument has a real appeal to certain sectors of American society.

For the final argument we return to Keynes's appeal to a vague and distant future where the gains of growth will be traded for leisure. This leisure is not well defined in the growth literature, but it does stand as one goal of economic activity and it exerts utopian drawing power. Seemingly, it is the deserved retirement for an economic system that has worked too hard in its productive years.

But, as Keynes concluded: "Beware!" Considerably more economic and technological growth will be necessary before material abundance is sufficient to trade work for leisure. That is, the quasi utopia of increased leisure is only possible through continued high rates of growth. Whether or not this vague utopia will ever be realized is not particularly important. It functions to give meaning and purpose to the economic and technological process. Herein lies its power as an argument.

The Critics Respond

The critics do not overlook the powerful thrust for growth nor the supporting role of the preceding arguments. They realize all too well the inevitable difficulties that result when growth slows down. In some cases they would offer alternatives—for example, a guaranteed annual income as one measure to alleviate the miseries of unemployment. They concede that there are difficulties in a reduced emphasis, especially in the area of international relations. Nor do they question the idealism of several of the arguments, notably the extra-product, the foreign-aid, and the leisure arguments. In principle, if not always in fact, they admit that these arguments make a good case for growth.

Nevertheless, the critics are not convinced that the preceding arguments should stand unchallenged. Among many criticisms, four in general stand out. First, critics point to the inconsistency between the ideal of the ethical arguments and what really happens in everyday life. Relatively little of the extra-product goes to the poor or to "real" social needs. Foreign aid is meager, indeed penurious. Leisure is not replacing work. These inconsistencies may be due to the technical difficulties of organizing effective programs. But a more likely view, according to the critics, is that the arguments in large part are a legitimating gloss for self-interest. That is to say, nations and individuals desire growth for selfish reasons. Humanitarian arguments merely disguise true motives and make a process devoted to mammon appear as if it is devoted to human well-being.

Second, critics maintain that advocates frequently overstate their case. To say that growth is necessary to maintain standards of living obscures the already high standards in most developed countries. To say that growth is necessary for jobs overlooks possible alternatives to present schemes of dealing with unemployment. To say that growth is essential to ensure military preparedness is incredibly myopic, given the already astronomical levels of military expenditure. The advocates make it seem as if growth were the only answer, when in many cases alternatives are available.

Third, some of the arguments have an imperialistic and nationalistic bias. The "demonstration effect" argument is preeminently of this sort. So also are the defense and the social strife arguments. The United States, according to some critics, is not out to win converts for capitalism, or to maintain the peace, but to ensure its dominant position and to provide safe havens for its imperialistic corporations.

Fourth, several of the arguments hide legitimate grievances, according to the critics. If growth helps to prevent social strife, it also blurs the important ethical issue of distribution. Insofar as growth has contributed to social harmony in the post–World War II period, it has also helped to perpetuate injustices that inevitably occur in periods of harmony. Indeed, the argument that everyone has more gives the illusion that the lot of the poor is improving, when in fact the gap between those who have and those who have not is widening. The poor still live in wretched conditions in America and throughout the world.

To conclude, we can observe that the arguments of the advocates make a fairly good case for growth. The case, though overstated and at points ethically problematic, is persuasive to large numbers throughout the world. Growth has produced real gains for human welfare and holds some promise for the future, especially in the less developed areas of the world. The social system is designed for growth, and to change it would probably entail great human suffering. These considerations, together with the factors in the thrust for growth, form something of a juggernaut whose direction and momentum will be difficult to alter, much less stop. In fact, in the absence of definitive proof that growth cannot continue, the forces in motion most likely will proceed with only minor modification and reform.

The Costs of Growth

"There is no such thing as a free lunch," is a sound economic principle. Behind every free lunch there are hidden costs to be taken into account. Translated for the growth debate by Barry Commoner, this principle

> is intended to warn that every gain is won at some cost. . . .
> Because the global ecosystem is a connected whole, in which
> nothing can be gained or lost and which is not subject to
> over-all improvement, anything extracted from it by human
> effort must be replaced. Payment of this price cannot be
> avoided; it can only be delayed. The present environment
> crisis is a warning that we have delayed nearly too long.[2]

Much has already been said in criticism of the present emphasis on economic growth. The real heart of the critics' position, however, is found in this issue of external or social costs. Economic growth involves substantial costs both to human beings and to the environment. These costs are frequently ignored by growth advocates, but they must be included, the critics insist. Any final reckoning of the desirability of growth must be measured against the two criteria of environmental soundness and human welfare.

The problem of social costs has a long history in discussions of the productive process, though indeed it has never been at the center of these discussions. In the literature of the advocates the problem of costs is occasionally encountered, but in general, references are scanty and not well developed. Consider, for example,

the following rather typical discussion by economist
Peter Gutmann:

> Economic growth has a number of costs: (1) Current leisure
> must be sacrificed for current work; (2) Current consump-
> tion of goods and services must be sacrificed in favor of
> provision for the future through savings and investment,
> research and development, and education; (3) Those who
> sacrifice current consumption are not always the same
> persons as those who benefit from increased provision for
> the future; (4) The stability and the predictable repetitive
> nature of an unchanging society must be sacrificed for the
> instabilities and uncertainties of economic growth.[3]

Other costs besides these have not been completely
ignored, yet until recently the focus has been narrow.
Not only have many costs been omitted, there has also
been a general feeling that social costs are peripheral
concerns and thus of little consequence. That costs will
be overcome through improved technologies or legislation is a common assumption. There has been, in short, a
pervasive optimism regarding costs.

The word "external," often used to designate these
costs, suggests how they have been viewed by most
advocates. They have been considered *outside* the normal computing of the costs of production. They have
been everybody's yet nobody's responsibility.

According to the critics, this narrow view of social
costs is myopic. It is rooted in a too-narrow perception
of what constitutes economic benefit. The uncritical
assumption that growth is good has led to an unwilling-
ness to face the political, ethical, and ideological implications of social costs. For the critics, these so-called
"external" costs must now be taken seriously, for the very

basis of economic and life systems is threatened. As for the advocates' analysis of costs in terms of consumption forgone, the critics hold that consumption forgone in a consumer society such as ours is meaningless. If the environmentally unsound patterns of the present continue, future consumption and welfare may well be less rather than greater.

In economic terms the critics are saying that the social cost of undifferentiated growth is now close to or exceeds the social benefit. In ecological terms they are saying that our productive processes are destroying important sectors of the ecosystem, the very sectors upon which the economy, growth or no growth, depends. In ethical terms they are saying that, on human and environmental grounds, undifferentiated growth is no longer desirable.

The costs of undifferentiated expansion have given rise to considerable recent commentary. Ecological impact studies have become popular. Without exhausting the many costs cited, the following are most frequently mentioned: (1) pollution—water, air, heat, noise; (2) depletion of irreplaceable natural resources; (3) various disamenities, such as traffic congestion, the neglect of many inner cities, the mounting quantity of trash, and temporary disruptions associated with construction; (4) several aesthetic costs, such as overhead power lines, the sameness of structures, noise, and urban sprawl; and (5) various human and political costs, including manipulative advertising, alienating work situations, the increased pace of industrial and urban life, the breakdown of the nuclear family, the domination of economic and technical values, the dislocations produced by rapid economic and technological change, and the role of growth in the perpetuation of inequality.

In almost every case, the critics claim, the market does not take these costs into account. According to K. William Kapp, these factors "do not enter into the cost calculations of private firms. They are shifted to and are paid for in one form or another by individuals other than the entrepreneur or by the community as a whole or by both." [4] As a result, the existing price system does not reflect the real costs of what we are buying and gives a relative advantage to industries that are able to pass these costs on to the public.

To the credit of the advocates, many are beginning to recognize these problems as serious. For the most part, however, they are still optimistic, confident that adjustments to existing structures, legislation, and increasing attention to technology can solve them. But, insist the critics, the problems are not merely technical and legal. They are also political and ethical. More important, they are products of a world view that structural or technical solutions alone will not alter. Consequently, there is no particular reason to trust the optimism of the advocates. The problems are more deeply rooted, the advocates' solutions mere palliatives.

How serious are these social costs? Is there really a crisis? Will technical solutions be sufficient? Unfortunately our crystal ball is cloudy. The "experts" are in fundamental disagreement through the whole range of social costs. To make matters worse, responses to these questions depend to a large extent on the basic values of the responder. So, without begging the issue, we must admit to being perplexed. Yes, there are serious problems. The abundance of commentary on costs attests to this. Yet, as a society we don't know how serious these social costs are. And we are far from making any fundamental change in direction.

Since the literature on costs is vast, a study of the ethical issues involved cannot hope to cover it. But it is instructive to consider the work of ecologist Barry Commoner. His book *The Closing Circle* is an excellent example of this literature. Not only does it detail the ecological costs of several forms of pollution, it also offers insight into causes. Commoner isolates a misdirected technological process as the primary culprit, and he brings into sharper focus the crucial differences between the advocates and their critics over the technological process.

Commoner's concern about pollution stems from his belief that the present pattern of environmental destruction in the United States threatens the very basis of the productive process itself—the ecosystem of the earth. The environmental crisis is both a sign that natural ecosystems have been overloaded and a warning that we need to discover why in order to take remedial action before the environment is destroyed.

To this question of the source of pollution Commoner directs a good deal of his attention. Where in the total of economic activities is it possible to find an explanation of the crisis?

Commoner first looks at the available evidence by considering several instances of significant pollution. Though inadequate, the evidence reveals that most pollution problems first appeared or became much worse in the years after World War II. That war, according to Commoner, represented something of a divide between the scientific revolution that preceded it and the technological revolution that followed. The postwar period represents the most rapid burst of technical creativity in human history. Could it be, he asks, that new technologies are the cause of environmental degradation?

Before exploring this hunch, Commoner investigates several alternative possibilities. First, he looks at population, which in the United States rose 42 percent between World War II and 1970. He rejects this as a primary cause. The increased production needed to feed, clothe, and house this increase might have caused a disproportionate rise in pollution due to inefficient means of production such as obsolete factories. But this would suggest no increase in efficiency, and would indicate zero or negative productivity gains, which has not been the American experience.[5] In fact, some of the worst polluters—for example, the chemical industry—have experienced the greatest productivity gains since World War II.

Commoner also rejects as a primary cause increased population density, an outstanding characteristic of postwar population growth, except as it has encouraged use of the automobile. In sum, the 42 percent increase in population and population density do not account for the 200 to 2,000 percent increase in environmental pollution.[6]

Next, Commoner considers "affluence" (rising GNP per capita) as a possible source. But GNP per capita rose only 50 percent in the period 1946–1966, an amount hardly sufficient to account for the much larger increases in pollution per capita. Indeed, the basics—clothing, food, shelter—did not increase significantly during the period. And while the per capita utilization of electric power, fuels, and paper products has increased, these increases hardly account for the striking rise in pollution levels.

Having rejected these two sources, Commoner reconsiders technology in a chapter entitled "The Technological Flaw." At the outset he again insists that economic growth in itself is not responsible for the sharp rise in environmental pollution. There is no theoretical reason why economic growth, strictly considered as rising GNP, must lead to pollution.[7] Rather, what is crucial is *how* growth is achieved. It can be ecologically unsound growth, such as the lumbering practiced by some firms that denudes hillsides and leads to soil erosion. Or a firm can practice soil conservation and replant forests, thus achieving sound growth.

So *how* has the economy grown? To answer this question Commoner considers the growth rates of several hundred production items. For each he has computed the average annual change in production or consumption for the years since 1946. At the top of the growth list was nonreturnable soda bottles, which increased 53,000 percent. Runners-up were synthetic fibers, 5,980 percent; mercury, 3,930 percent; air conditioners, 4,850 percent; plastics, 1,960 percent; nitrogen fertilizers, 1,050 percent; synthetic organic chemicals, 950 percent; aluminum, 630 percent; electric power, 530 percent; pesticides, 390 percent; truck freight, 222 percent; and motor fuel consumption, 190 percent.[8]

Technology emerges as the prime polluter of the environment. The vaunted "progress" of postwar technological innovations has been the main cause. The effect: environmental pollution has increased at a rate ten times that of the GNP and has been largely borne not by the consumers or producers but by nearby neighbors and society at large.

Another fact emerges. Many of the new technologies

consume more electrical power and fuel-generated energy per unit of production than those they replaced. For example, aluminum as a substitute for steel requires considerably more power to produce. In terms of the environment, aluminum is less efficient than steel. Of course, the environmental costs have not been figured into the costs of production, a fact that makes environmentally unsound growth appear relatively cheap. The costs of environmental destruction are borne by the anonymous many or put off to future generations. Nor have the implications of this substitution for resource depletion been considered.

Commoner concludes:

> The over-all evidence seems clear. The chief reason for the environmental crisis that has engulfed the United States in recent years is the sweeping transformation of productive technology since World War II. The economy has grown enough to give the United States population about the same amount of basic goods, per capita, as it did in 1946. However, productive technologies with intense impacts on the environment have displaced less destructive ones. The environmental crisis is the inevitable result of this counter-ecological pattern of growth.[9]

The fault, according to Commoner, lies with the way our society has elected to gain, distribute, and use its wealth. The crisis, in other words, is social and political, not just technical.

The reasons for the technological flaw are not hard to uncover. One primary cause is that the technologist defines his problem too narrowly. He takes into his purview only one segment of what in nature is an endless cycle that can collapse with overstress at a few points.

According to Commoner, technologists have "tubular vision."

Moreover, pollution problems have arisen not from minor inadequacies in the new technologies, but from the very fact that they were so successful. They are not failures when measured against their stated aims. The problem is in the aim. The aim is too narrow, largely because the technological process, including its scientific foundation, forces the division and subdivision of each task into component parts. It loses sight of the whole. But the ecosystem, in contrast, cannot be divided into parts. Its essential properties reside in the whole, and a process that deals only in parts is bound to fail.

With all this, it is important to note that Commoner does not reject science-based technology. He does not condemn science and technology merely because they are the primary cause of environmental degradation. Rather, he insists that there is a social and ecological basis to science and technology. He would opt for a technological process that is much more concerned about side effects on the environment and on human welfare. The environmental crisis tells us that certain costs are not being paid directly, and that certain groups, in particular the poor, are the main losers.

How would Commoner correct the current pattern of economic and technological growth? On the surface the solution appears simple. Since pollution is a result in varying degrees of population increase, affluence, and especially the "technological flaw," it is necessary to consider all three. But it seems clear from what has preceded that making technology environmentally sound would be the best approach. This is not to say, however, that population control isn't necessary on other grounds.

Interestingly, Commoner rejects the idea of consuming less. Not only would the impact of lowered consumption on the environment be relatively insignificant compared to a correction of the technological flaw, but, more important to Commoner, such action seems hardly sensible in the face of widespread poverty and need. While by no means rejecting new ecological life-styles, he seems to imply in his remarks not that we should produce and consume less, but that we should produce and consume less of certain things.

Finally, Commoner turns to the economic implications of his insights. If the main task is to correct the present environmentally unsound pattern of growth, the fundamental question is this: Are the basic operational requirements of the private enterprise and socialist economic systems compatible with ecological imperatives? Phrasing it another way: Can the environmental costs, which at present are largely not included, be brought into the price system?

Many economists think the inclusion of environmental costs is possible. However, if such an inclusion results in closing down certain productive activities because they are too costly, a number of people will suffer and there is no guarantee that others will gain. Moreover, the industries so affected will in all likelihood resist such inclusion. Indeed, the problem is even more complex. According to Commoner, it is the new technologies that have played an important role in making postwar business profitable. We can add that they have also been of crucial significance to the growth process itself.

The role that new technology plays in the growth process is clear. New technology usually increases productivity (more output per unit of input). Increased productivity in turn leads to less cost per unit which, in the absence of other cost-producing factors, will lead to greater profits. This suggests that the motive behind the introduction of polluting technologies in the postwar period was profits. Available evidence seems to confirm this, at least in the capitalistic countries. Chemical manufacturers earned greater profits than the average for all manufacturing industries until 1966 when, according to their own accounts, environmental considerations led to a marked decline in profits. Larger, more environmentally destructive automobiles yield higher profits. Aluminum, cement, and plastics, with higher profit margins, were often substituted for steel and lumber, with lower profit margins. More profitable detergents were substituted for less profitable soaps.

Not all the new technologies have led to greater environmental pollution. An outstanding exception is the substitution of oil-burning diesel engines for coal-steam locomotion. Significantly, this gain has not been exploited for the transportation of people. But the point is that environmentally destructive technological substitutions have been far more numerous. This leads Commoner to conclude that, while increased profitability does not inevitably lead to increased pollution, "many of the heavily polluting new technologies have brought with them a higher rate of profit than the less polluting technologies they have displaced." [10]

Nevertheless, Commoner makes too much of the profitability factor. His analysis does not explain pollution in socialist economies. And while profits are no doubt important, Galbraith and many others make clear that large corporations do not always try to maximize profits. They seek profits to a point, but then other goals come into play. Hence Commoner's statement, "Driven by an inherent tendency to maximize profits, modern private enterprise has seized upon those massive technological innovations that promise to gratify this need . . . ," is too strong and, once again, reductionistic.[11]

Other forces, perhaps even more powerful, are also at work. All those factors which have combined to produce the strong thrust for economic growth regardless of its content are operative. This thrust has been narrow. It has excluded noneconomic and nontechnological values. It has diverted attention from the distribution question and from the cost question as well. It has led, in short, to an indiscriminate use of environmentally destructive new technologies. Thus, while Commoner rests his case on profits, perhaps it is more correct to say that profits are one of several factors in the overall thrust.

Now, if the causes of pollution and other social costs are complex, the corrective process will undoubtedly be difficult. The inclusion of social costs in the price system runs counter to the direction of the growth thrust at many points. Inclusion of social costs will probably reduce profits because of lowered productivity. But this is just the start. It may also call into question the efficacy of technology, reduce consumption alternatives, increase unemployment, force a rise in taxes, place greater restrictions on the autonomy of the technostructure, raise questions of social justice, and disturb the political order. The task will certainly be more difficult than a mere call for nonpolluting technologies. It will involve social, political, ideological, and ethical considerations, which are considerably more difficult for societies to handle.

In summarizing the insights of Commoner for the

growth debate, we should point first to his most important contribution, the isolation of new technologies and their scientific basis as the primary cause of environmental pollution. Pollution is, of course, only one of many social costs cited earlier, but it is characteristic of many others. Second, Commoner has exposed the higher fuel consumption of new technologies and the implication this has for pollution and resource depletion. Third, he has revealed how deeply pollution costs are woven into the present economic and technological fabric. Fourth, Commoner has pointed out that pollution costs and their elimination are not merely technical problems. They involve social, political, and ethical considerations—though, indeed, he has insufficiently developed this theme. Fifth, he has shown that social costs and the few attempts to pay these costs have been borne disproportionately by the poor. Finally, Commoner has made clear that growth need not be environmentally destructive, that a distinction between environmentally sound growth and destructive growth is possible.

Proposed Solutions to the Problem of Social Costs

The obvious solution to the problem of social costs would be to include them in the price paid for an item or in the accounting systems of economic units in which they originate. This sounds simple enough, but the practical difficulties are considerable. In addition to those already noted, there is the difficulty that many of the costs are impossible to measure, much less to price.

Both critics and advocates agree that social costs ought to be included in the cost accounting process.

Almost no one favors continuing environmental degradation. The rub comes with balancing the "good" of economic growth against its negative impact. No one advocates the elimination of all social costs by stopping production, just as no one supports the disregard of human and environmental effects by giving *carte blanche* to growth.

The advocates would tilt the balance in the direction of growth, the critics in the direction of the environment. Both would say that individuals and society benefit more from having it in their preferred direction.

Equally important, the two groups differ on the means of achieving balance. The advocates emphasize solutions that involve technology, substitution, and minor price manipulation. They seek an "efficient" solution. They are also relatively confident that such solutions will produce the desired effect without the need of rigid controls. In contrast, the critics point to certain limitations of the technological process itself, and to the political, ethical, and attitudinal changes that are necessary before the technical solutions can be effectively applied. They generally are more willing to accept coercive solutions.

In spite of these differences there are some areas in which the two sides generally agree. Accurate data on social costs are needed; the technology as well as the costs and benefits of proposed projects should be publicly assessed; "clean" technologies must be found to replace "dirty" ones; manipulations of tax structures and price systems are preferred to more drastic, coercive measures; more durable products and recycling of materials are desirable; and in some cases stringent laws may be required.

So what can we say about Keynes's hope for his grandchildren? Do we side with the advocates who still believe that the growth process increases the range of human choice and improves the quality of life? Or do we side with the critics who claim that the harmful effects of the growth process, as we know it, outweigh the benefits? Or perhaps this either/or alternative is too simplistic. With a few advocates, we may wish to reform the growth process, leaving the basic system intact. Or with some critics, we may merely wish to include the most noxious social costs within the accounting systems.

Arnold Toynbee, in an essay in the *New York Times,* made this query: "Is the proper goal of human life the glorification of God and the enjoyment of Him forever? Or is it the maximization of mankind's gross global material wealth?" For the Christian this is a crucial question. But, like most either/or's, it fails to do justice to the gray area in between. What would Toynbee say to the Third World's poor, who still have much to gain from an increase in global material prosperity? Could it be, as the advocates suggest, that increasing material wealth and enjoyment of God are complementary, or at the very least not incompatible?

Many Christians, hearing the debate over growth, side with the critics and quickly draw the conclusion that Americans are too materialistic, too dedicated to the mammon of perpetual material increase. But this judgment is too easy because the growth process is ethically more ambiguous. Even with its oppressive and idolatrous ideology it has in fact produced remarkable benefits for many and may continue to do so.

Reality is almost always more complex than simple solutions suggest. While it is easy to render judgment on

American materialism using the spirituality and love of Jesus as a plumb line, let us withhold our judgment for a while. Let us explore some of the more prominent ethical issues first, and attempt to review the broad scope of this complex and ambiguous question before we take sides.

Chapter 5

THREE
ETHICAL ISSUES

Charges of insensitivity to the poor and oppressed punctuate the debate between advocates and critics. It would seem at times as if this concern was the central preoccupation of each group. Needless to say, such claims should arouse our suspicion. Yet, behind the moral posturing lurks an extremely important ethical question: how equitably are the benefits of growth distributed?

Distribution

Growth advocates are aware of the "wide" differentials in the distribution of income and wealth in the United States.[1] These differentials are remarkably constant throughout the industrialized world. Generally the advocates are not too bothered by the statistical evidence of inequality. Some are unconcerned. Others argue that growth reduces inequality. Still others say that growth is the only possible way to alleviate poverty.

To sort out these arguments we must first deal with a

potential source of confusion. The growth process produces more for everyone. Each piece of pie keeps getting bigger. But this does not necessarily mean that the percentage of the total pie is also getting bigger. Actually, it may be increasing, remaining the same, or decreasing. We should therefore not assume that dwindling numbers below an arbitrarily defined poverty line mean greater equality of income and wealth. Growth, which does in fact produce more for everyone, does not necessarily lead to greater equality of distribution.

Historical evidence on income and wealth indicates that inequalities narrow in the early stages of industrialization. On the basis of this selective evidence a few advocates hold that the growth process makes relative shares more equal. But the evidence is not altogether convincing. While narrowing does occur, it seems to go only so far. For countries in the more advanced stages of industrialization there is little evidence of continued narrowing.

Most advocates of growth do not dwell on this historical evidence. They point instead to the obvious fact that growth eliminates absolute poverty. Economist Robert Lampman argues:

> The growth in per capita income in the postwar period has resulted in a substantial reduction of the number and percent of persons in poverty. The decline from 12 million to 9.3 million families with less than $3,000 incomes of 1962 purchasing power is a signal accomplishment of our economy. To continue this reduction is a prime reason for encouraging further economic growth. If we can continue the 1947–1962 rate of growth, the number of poor families should decline to 7 million, or 12 percent of all families by 1975.

While growth in per capita income and production is not the only factor in the reduction of poverty, it is clear that the rate of reduction responds to changes in the rate of growth. Between 1947 and 1957, when per capita income grew at a rate of 3 percent per year, the percent of families in poverty fell from 32 to 23. Between 1957 and 1962, when income grew at a rate of only 2 percent, the percent in poverty fell only from 23 to 20 percent.

Nevertheless, Lampman is forced to amend his argument in the face of mounting evidence that much remaining poverty is immune to the growth process.

It is true that there are some groups in poverty, most notably the aged and broken families, who are relatively immune to economic growth because they are not part of the labor force. For these groups, growth will make only indirect contributions. It will produce the public revenues which are necessary for higher social insurance and public assistance benefits whereby poverty can be relieved.[2]

In other words, we have reached a dead end. Growth alone is not the cure. Remaining poverty can only be attacked through selective programs that divert the extra-product of growth in the direction of the poor. This is not to say growth is irrelevant. According to Lampman it makes selective programs more feasible. And to this we might add that the cessation of growth under present conditions would be catastrophic for the poor.

Other advocates maintain that some inequality is necessary for the smooth functioning of the economic system. Inequality is a by-product of a system that benefits rich and poor alike. Individuals must be rewarded for taking risks, for assuming responsibility, for providing a scarce commodity, or for exploiting a profitable investment. Otherwise the system stagnates and unemployment results. Indeed, even if some persons are rewarded out of proportion to their contribution, all benefit either directly or indirectly through such things as increased employment and better public services. To follow this line of argument through, efforts to redistribute will inevitably depress the system and are likely to hurt the poor worst of all. Moreover, redistribution would require coercive measures antithetical to the freedoms we cherish.

Still other advocates point to the technical and political difficulties that would be associated with redistribution. Historically, points out British economist J. R. Hicks, redistribution has provided little to the poor in the way of increased income and wealth.[3]

Anthony Crosland, a Labour M.P. who has consistently argued the case of the poor, emphasizes the political difficulties.[4] He claims that redistribution by fiat is practically impossible in most Western democracies for political reasons alone. Redistribution would require higher taxation and certain forms of public spending, such as family allowances and supplementary benefits, both of which would encounter intense and acrimonious opposition especially in periods of no growth or slow growth.

Above all, Crosland sees that under present conditions any political party advocating a major redistribution program would probably lose the next election. In addition, though he doesn't mention it, there also seems to be a general distaste for the coercive measures that such a redistribution would require. Crosland thus writes off direct attempts at redistribution as politically infeasible. In part, also, he writes off direct efforts because he feels that economic growth can accomplish the same thing.

Finally, nearly all advocates claim international redistribution magnifies the technical and political problems several times over. When wealth lies primarily in productive capacity or resources, it is no simple matter to make transfers, as the Russians learned in their efforts to relocate German industry after World War II.

In sum, according to these arguments, growth and at least some differentials in wealth and income are necessary for the poor to prosper. Responses that are ethically concerned with the plight of the poor must recognize and accept this.

The critics do not deny the technical and political difficulties of redistribution. Rather than emphasize these, they focus on the persistence of inequality. They stress the immunity of remaining poverty to the growth cure and urge the enactment of selective programs for the poor instead of reliance on growth. The critics also question the degree of disturbance that redistribution would create; the seeming "naturalness" of present inequalities; the significance of the technical and political obstacles that stand in the way of redistribution; and the havoc that a slowed growth rate would wreak on the poor. In particular, the last is a point of contention. Many critics believe that redistribution would help to alleviate the dislocations and unemployment resulting from a slowed growth rate. Perhaps that puts it too mildly. It may be that without redistribution the payment of social costs and serious attention to the problems of resource scarcity would be impossible because of political conflict. If the poorer are forced to sacrifice while the richer hardly feel the pinch, the stage is set for intense political strife. There can be no real peace unless social costs are shared, and they cannot be shared without some narrowing of inequalities of income and wealth.

For the critics concerned about the poor, perhaps the major objection is the degree to which growth has blunted the ethical imperative for redistribution. Growth, they contend, has obscured the distribution question. This has been the result of stressing the increasing numbers of persons who have risen above an arbitrarily chosen and much too low "poverty level" and of emphasizing rising levels of consumption. No one has worried much about relative pieces of pie as long as everyone's piece was growing. As a result, an "unjust" distribution of wealth has been perpetuated to the disadvantage of the poor.

Not only has growth blunted the ethical imperative, it has also produced complacency about the poverty that remains. "Why worry about the poor? Enough will trickle down to relieve their misery." Yet millions remain in misery. The bulk of the extra-product has gone to the middle and upper classes. The "welfare program" for the rich has been incredibly generous,[5] while tiny sums for the poor have been parceled out begrudgingly and in dehumanizing ways. The deterioration of the inner cities and of mass transit, as well as the shocking state of the criminal justice system, are just a few fruits of this complacency and "benign" neglect. From these criticisms it is easy to see in the arguments of the advocates an elaborate ideological framework to perpetuate the existing distribution.

Why is this issue of distribution so hotly debated? Primarily because the continuing wide differentials in wealth and income and the neglect of the issue since World War II are intolerable to many on both sides. Beyond this the issue has powerful political ramifications. Both sides want to avoid the telling criticism of insensitivity to the poor. In an effort to enlist the support of organizations involved in other causes, both groups want to appear ethically sensitive. This need for political alliance is particularly strong for the critics, who are clearly in a minority and are sometimes cast as insensitive for preferring trees to people. Many critics realize that little will be done on environmental problems as long as the environmentalist's interests are seen as being in opposition to the worker's.

These considerations again point to the future. If the problem of social costs is ever faced or if growth grinds to a halt because of natural limits, the issue of distribution will be unavoidable. In a time of sacrifice the inequalities will be too glaring. For anything to be accomplished, either redistribution or totalitarian rule will be necessary.

Thus the issue of distribution is crucial to the debate. It is important therefore to probe the ethical basis for determining when a given distribution of income and wealth is maldistribution.

For the Christian the starting point of an adequate approach is not statistics, but the obvious concern in both Old and New Testaments for those at the bottom of society. In speaking of God's perfect righteousness, Paul Ramsey has summarized this concern:

> Biased in favor of the helpless, "justice" means care for the poor, the orphans, the widows, and alien residents in the land. . . . Righteousness requires that the sojourner in the land of promise be cared for, even as God cared for Israel during the days of sojourning in Egypt when he

unexpectedly and without their meriting it saved them from slavery.[6]

This concern should at least place the Christian on guard against any distribution in which unequal portions result in the absolute or relative misery of those at the bottom. Involved in this concern is the liberation of the poor and oppressed, a demand for justice, a deeply felt compassion for the condition of poverty, and a call to generous sharing. Above all in the teachings of Jesus there is a sensitivity toward the poor, both the poor in worldly goods and the poor in spirit. However, it is a concern that has no illusions about the poor and does not idealize them. Like all other persons, the poor are made in the image of God and exist in a condition of sin and estrangement.

Moreover, through Jesus Christ each person is called to a responsible relationship of love to God and to neighbor. Herein, however, lies a difficulty. Love presupposes a relatively intimate relation of person to person, a closeness that can take into account the ambiguities of the situation and the varying needs of the neighbor. Such love is only a partial possibility in a world of billions. The structures of modern states do not love and are too complex to be administered on the basis of love. As a result, several schools of Christian ethical thought have appealed to the norm of justice as the working out of love in more complex social situations. Here the Christian tradition joins in dialogue with Western political philosophy.

Justice may be broken down into two regulative principles—liberty and equality—which serve as critical standards for order and distribution. For the distribution of income and wealth, the regulative principle of equality is the more important.

Both the Christian and the Western philosophical traditions recognize the equality of worth in each individual. What the principle of equality asserts is that no human being shall have an advance claim to better treatment or greater privilege than another. That is, the starting point is equality. Departures from equality place the burden of proof on the person or group that would distort equality. It does not mean that all persons are equal in fact or that justice demands egalitarianism. Rather, the only ethical ground for treating persons differently is that they differ in some respect that is relevant to the inequality that is proposed. The principle of equality is thus a norm prescribing that inequalities of income and wealth are not justified under any circumstances until relevant grounds for them are established. To act in a just manner means, therefore, to treat all persons alike except where differences are relevant and significant.

The regulative principle of equality includes two subprinciples: (1) relevance, which seeks to distinguish between criteria of difference offered in support of a given inequality, and (2) proportionality, which states that only a limited amount of inequality is justifiable, this limit representing in some rough way the degree of relevance.

It should come as no surprise that social organizations do not embody these principles perfectly and never will. In reality what is usually taken for justice is a balance with the actual distribution largely reflecting the relative power of individuals and groups to command income and wealth. The relation of the principles to actual conditions is one of moral influence. The principles influence negatively by bringing the existing balance into question; positively by suggesting the direction a more just balance might take. These principles do in fact exert this influence. Existing realities are modified as persons and groups allow their behavior to be influenced by such ethical norms as justice and equality. Thus a cynical "might makes right" type of justice is seldom encountered, and societies in varying degrees do approximate these norms.

In addition to the idealism of the principles and the realism of power balances there is a further element. Persons and groups approach the problem of distribution as they approach any ethical problem. They come to it with a world view on the basis of which they judge whether existing conditions are just or not. The world view, in other words, is the real basis of judgment. It largely determines whether or not challenges will be made to the existing distribution. It puts meat, so to speak, on the bones of the formal concept of justice. Nevertheless, while most ethical judgments are made on the basis of pre-given world views, persons and groups in varying degrees are able to modify their views to encompass more of the ideal.

To summarize, there are three primary elements in an ethical approach to the question of distribution. First there is the normative element. For the Christian, this includes a clear concern for the poor; a call for love, compassion, sensitivity, and justice in personal and social relationships with the poor; and a set of rational principles. Second there is the existing distribution system, which represents a balance of power modified to a certain extent by moral considerations. Third there is the world view, the attitudes, perceptions, and understandings that provide a framework and give content to the normative and real elements. With these three elements it will now be possible to evaluate the present distribution of income and wealth in the United States.

The present distribution system represents no particular problem for many, perhaps the great majority of Americans. They perceive no gross conflict in their world views between the facts of the distribution and the principles of love and justice. Yet the fact that they perceive no problem does not mean that the existing system embodies love and justice to any great degree.

The existing distribution of income in the United States is primarily a result of the job one holds and secondarily of the profits, interest, rent, and various forms of transfer payments one receives. Wealth is distributed primarily through earnings and inheritance.

The important question here, however, is not the channels through which income and wealth are pumped. Rather it is the reasons put forward and accepted for inequality in the actual distribution of income and wealth.

Without claiming to be complete and discrete, we can identify fourteen criteria: (1) quantity of work, (2) status, (3) unpleasantness of job, (4) luck or chance, (5) intelligence or ability, (6) education, (7) need, (8) supply of and demand for specific occupations, (9) responsibility, (10) ownership, (11) risk, (12) productivity, (13) inheritance, and (14) family connections. Let us examine the first criterion. Extra income for extra work is held to be a justifiable departure from equality on the grounds that work incentives are a necessary element of any functioning economy. It is also justified by the principle of equality and the subprinciple of proportionality. That is, equal amounts of work should receive equal pay, unequal amounts unequal pay proportionate to the amount of work.

To take another example, the ownership of property is singled out as a source of departure from equality on the grounds of incentive. Property ownership is also justified on the grounds that it is necessary for the efficient operation of our market economy and that it helps to preserve basic freedoms. In a similar manner attempts can be made to justify each of the fourteen criteria.

As these examples show, every relevant criterion has a rationale behind it. In discussions of income and wealth there are seven rationales frequently encountered, all of which, except the sixth and the seventh, assume a functioning economic system. They are: (1) efficiency; (2) stability; (3) growth and productivity; (4) incentive; (5) preservation of the market system; (6) freedom of individuals to acquire and dispose; and, on occasion, (7) equality.

The question now becomes whether these criteria and their accompanying rationales are acceptable on Christian ethical grounds as relevant departures from equality. Some would want to say that the only relevant departure is human need. Such a position is certainly supportable by the ethical rigor of portions of the New Testament. Yet many Christians would be willing to admit certain other departures on the basis of what Max Weber has called an ethic of responsibility. For example, all other variables being equal, there is ethical justification for distributing twice as much pay to a person who works twice as many hours in the same job.

Many Christians would even be willing to admit the criteria that derive their relevance from the requirements of economic systems as long as the principle of proportionality is strictly observed and functional importance is clearly established. That is to say, there is some measure of ethical justification for any economic system that maintains stability and distributes rewards with some measure of efficiency. For any economic system to function, some system of incentives must be established. Hence some departure from equality is admissible on incentive grounds. Incentive criteria have a derivative relevancy.

Without going further into the complexities of each criterion and rationale, we can make several ethical criticisms of the departures from equality commonly accepted in the United States and of the distribution of income and wealth that has resulted.

First, several criteria that are the most justifiable on Christian grounds have but little effect on the existing distribution. Most prominent are the quantity of work, the relative unpleasantness of a given occupation, and the need for survival and some measure of economic dignity. Time spent on a job is a minor source of inequality. Some jobs receive higher pay because they are hazardous or subject to extreme weather conditions or simply unpleasant. But this is by no means the rule for most jobs. As for appeals to basic necessities, these have produced welfare systems that prevent starvation in most industrial countries. Nevertheless, welfare serves more as a brake preventing the poor from getting poorer. In no way is it a major source of inequality. We may conclude from this that the case for current inequalities is measurably weakened if these, the most ethically viable grounds for departure, are of little or no consequence to the existing distribution.

Second, several of the criteria are irrelevant ethically as justifications yet have a significant impact on existing inequality. They are status, luck or chance, and family connections. Despite its long history in Western society as an acceptable justification, status is an appeal to pride, not love, and denies equality of worth. Luck or chance and family connections in turn are concessions to a determinism that denies the basis of ethical decision. Again the existing distribution, because it reflects these irrelevant criteria and is justified by them, loses another measure of ethical support.

Third, the bulk of the criteria, especially incentive criteria, have only a derivative relevancy. They are required, or thought to be required, for the efficient functioning of the economic system. They are not to be minimized on this account, for any functioning economic system has some ethical justification. But we must ask with the critics of growth to what degree Americans have conceded to their economic system an importance out of proportion to its ethical justification as a means to the end of material well-being. We must ask further to what degree the narrow focus of the economic system has obscured other value considerations. In short, to what extent do Americans give over the determination of distribution to an impersonal, conservative, and deterministic system and thereby sacrifice an element of their freedom?

Many Christians and critics of growth believe that Americans have conceded far too much to economic criteria in the determination of social policy. They also believe that the criteria which derive their relevancy from the necessities of the economic system are overstated.

Take for example the criterion of individual ability. This criterion provides little if any independent ethical justification in the distribution of income and wealth. Ability depends in large measure on genetic inheritance, upbringing, and education, the range of available opportunities, and an indeterminate amount of freedom to manipulate one's environment. None of these in itself provides ethical justification for departures from equality of income and wealth. Relative ability, however, is justified as a relevant criterion with the rationale that efficient and dynamic social systems must provide incentive to encourage the able to exploit their talents. Herein lies the relevancy of the ability criterion.

The values of efficiency and dynamism are given emphasis out of proportion to other values. Because they are, the rewards for abilities that contribute to the system are also overstated. In other words, society rewards ability more than other equally important, noneconomic criteria. As a result, the existing distribution is skewed more than the principle of proportionality justifies.

Fourth, moving into more general considerations, the world view that accepts these criteria and rationales is dominated by economic considerations, according to many critics. This world view is an ideology in which the primary goal is economic and technological expansion. The needs of the poor and considerations of equality play little part in it. Consequently, the fact that existing departures are considered relevant should come as no surprise. Nevertheless, this acceptance should not stand as a justifying rationale. Against the ethical standards already set forth, the world views that currently dominate the culture overstate the relevancy and the proportionality of departures from equality on economic grounds.

Fifth, in the present distribution of income and wealth little emphasis is given to the principle of proportionality. The primary method of implementing this principle is through the tax system. But the tax system in the United States has little if any redistributive effects. Proportionality is, of course, observed to a degree through the countervailing power of labor unions, minimum wage legislation, and some welfare programs. Yet these either exclude large numbers of the poor or benefit the rich more than the poor. Even the graduated income tax, certainly one of the most important efforts to observe proportionality, seems to have little effect, except perhaps as a counterbalance to the regressive nature of the rest of the tax structure. On these grounds the conclusion is reached that the principle of proportionality is largely ignored.

Sixth, that the existing distribution has been challenged so infrequently in recent years attests to how little even the principle of relevancy is actually considered. In fact the burden of proof has shifted to those who would depart from existing inequalities. This is a curious reversal of basic ethical theory in which the norm of justice places the burden of proof on departures from equality, not on departures from the *status quo*. What has actually occurred is a rough balance of power in which the given distribution has been accepted as an approximation of equality. As a result, those who advocate greater equality are forced to establish relevancy. Such a state of affairs cannot be justified on ethical grounds.

Seventh, the existing distribution of income and

wealth in the United States falls far short of the mark when considered against the Biblical concern for the poor. The documented evidence of great poverty in the midst of plenty and of public neglect in the midst of private affluence is ample testimony to the shocking neglect of the poor in America. Nor can the racial basis of existing poverty be overlooked.

From these criticisms it is possible to define more adequately the term "maldistribution." Maldistribution is a distribution of income and wealth in which:

1. Relevant ethical criteria for departures from equality are of little significance.
2. Irrelevant criteria dominate.
3. Deterministic and impersonal factors other than those required by a functioning economic system are allowed to widen markedly the distribution.
4. No conscious effort is made to assess proportionality.
5. The question of relevancy is largely ignored.
6. Little effort is made to correct inequalities through a progressive tax system.
7. The burden of establishing relevancy is shifted to those who would have greater equality.
8. The poor are neglected and poverty exists in the midst of plenty.
9. The public sector is allowed to deteriorate in the midst of private affluence.
10. Racial discrimination is an important source of inequalities.

When a significant number of these factors are present in the actual distribution of income and wealth, maldistribution exists.

Against this definition consider the following assessment by economist Burton A. Weisbrod:

> The income distribution in the United States depends largely on the outcome of forces operating through the private market. At its most efficient "best," the private market rewards people in accordance with their contribution to marketable output which, in turn, reflects consumer preferences and incomes. This implies that persons whose productivity, in value terms, is low will earn little—regardless of whether productivity is attributable to lack of effort, lack of skill, or low demand for the skill.
>
> The market rewards output, not effort. People who lack education and training, persons with limited intellectual ability or poor health, people producing goods and services for which the supply is so large relative to the demand that very low prices result—all of these are likely to earn little. By contrast, those with greater ability, more and better education and training, and having skills that are in relatively short supply will tend to earn more, perhaps even when working shorter hours and under more attractive conditions. . . .
>
> In addition, discrimination . . . has the effect of not fully rewarding people for their actual productivity, or not permitting them to obtain jobs in which their productivity would be maximized.[7]

The available evidence concerning income and wealth and an analysis of the existing distribution seems to support the conclusion that maldistribution exists in the United States.

This conclusion, when coupled with the failure of Americans to turn their extra-products toward social needs and the poor, lends considerable weight to the view that growth covers over injustice. This is not to say that the poor have gone empty-handed. Some of the fruits of growth have certainly trickled down, as Robert Lampman contends. Also, it is highly unlikely that real change will occur in our distribution pattern. Thus the best hope of the poor may still lie with growth. Growth, however, is not the "golden egg" that its supporters claim. The growth process, while producing benefits, is also an ideological cover. With or without growth, poverty remains a problem and redistribution an ethical imperative.

What about the distribution of social costs? It is now widely assumed that the future costs of reversing environmental degradation will be borne disproportionately by the poor. In the absence of mitigating programs, the poor will be the first and hardest hit by higher prices, increased unemployment, and regressive tax systems. What is frequently overlooked, however, is the degree to which the unpaid social costs of current environmental deterioration are already disproportionately borne by the poor.

In the absence of reliable information, propositions about the distribution of current social costs cannot be conclusively demonstrated. Nevertheless, the circumstantial evidence seems clear. It is not the rich who live near industrial parks, downwind from polluting factories, or in the slums of our cities. It is not the rich who have no other alternative except the local polluted beach for summer recreation. To put it bluntly, the wealthier a man is, the easier it is to force the disamenities in one way or another on the poor, or to avoid them altogether.

The growth process, while not an immediate cause, has contributed to this maldistribution. The growth process directs available investment funds into the most profitable areas. Consequently, the cities and the poor found in them are left to pick up the crumbs. This means they must contend with higher incidences of diseases, higher levels of pollution, and neglected transit systems. Usually the poor pay more for less. John Kenneth Galbraith has stated the situation simply:

> In slums, it has long been recognized, there is no socially useful market response. Rents, because of demand for space, tend to be at the highest level the traffic will bear. Being at the maximum, they will be no higher if the property is replaced, improved or even decently maintained. The most profitable course is to minimize outlay and, where possible, to pack more people in.[8]

Will the costs of an improved environment fall disproportionately on the poor? The answer is obvious. Of course they will, unless programs are enacted to redistribute these costs. To argue that corrective costs would fall disproportionately on the poor is no defense for allowing undifferentiated growth or for putting off measures to improve the environment. The poor pay either way. They may in fact only be trading one "cost" for another.

The distribution of income, wealth, and social costs is a problem whether or not there is economic growth and whether or not the environment is protected. The normal functioning of the market system must be tampered with if an equitable distribution is to be attained. To relieve the poor or near-poor of their disproportionate share of corrective costs it is necessary to enact specific legislation that will more equitably distribute the costs. To effect any change in the present distribution of costs it is necessary to enact such legislation. From an ethical point of view there is no way to avoid the distribution question. The big problem with including social costs in the present cost accounting system is to ensure that the poor will not pay more.

Who Should Pay?

Economist Edwin G. Dolan has offered an interesting hypothetical situation:

> Suppose that in a certain small community a chemical processing plant is emitting a strong, evil odor which pervades the entire town. It is always difficult to put a cash value on the damage caused in such a case, but, judging by the amount of money people spend to pamper their nostrils with deodorants, perfumes, aerosols, incense, and flowers, let us conservatively assume that each of the 1000 residents of this community would think it a bargain to be rid of the nuisance for as little as $10. Suppose further that the cost of scrubbing and filtering equipment at the plant which would entirely suppress the odor is estimated at $6000. What is to be done?
>
> Clearly . . . an opportunity for mutual beneficial action to remove the source of the inefficiency exists. Each citizen of the town could contribute $6 to a general fund, to present the factory owner with a big crate of scrubbing and filtering equipment. Each citizen would thus profit to the extent of $4 (since they would get rid of a $10 nuisance at the bargain price of $6), and the owner would have lost nothing.[9]

But why should the victims of air pollution pay the polluter, asks Dolan, even if it is to their advantage to do so? Aren't the owners of the plant at fault? Do not simple canons of justice demand that the costs of cleaning up be borne by the one creating the mess?

The answers to these questions are not easy. If mutual accommodation and self-sacrifice are abandoned as alternatives by the victims of pollution, a conflict situation is likely. The advantage in most cases is with the polluter. Not only does the factory owner usually have a financial advantage; he is also likely to have allies. Customers faced with a potential price rise necessitated by the increased costs of cleanup will testify on behalf of the polluter. Likewise, if prices cannot be raised, it may be necessary to cut production and lay off workers. The workers, faced with this prospect, will also join ranks with the factory owner.

This, of course, does not change the ethics of the situation. The factory owner has been able to keep his price low by passing on the environmental costs in the form of pollution. Likewise, his customers and workers have shared in and benefited from this hidden subsidy. As a result, they too should pay the costs of cleanup.

Dolan himself opts for passing the costs of pollution abatement on to the customer in the form of price increases. Disposal of wastes resulting, for example, from the manufacture of a car is just as much an operating expense as buying gasoline and tires. We should expect the car owner to bear such costs. But Dolan's solution, however sound in theory, once again overlooks the distribution question. Barry Commoner makes this quite clear.

> Consider . . . the often proposed idea that the costs of environmental control or improvement can be met by "passing them along to the consumer." Suppose, as predicted, the cost of exhaust controls adds several hundred dollars to the price of a car. To the rich person who buys an expensive car, the added expense is easily borne; but to the poor person the added cost may make the difference between having a car or none.[10]

This solution also overlooks the real suffering that would accompany any large-scale unemployment resulting from the reduced demand of higher prices. It may seem that the workers are guilty of benefiting at the expense of others and should, therefore, accept their part of the burden of reparations. But in most cases it is not their design to harm their neighbors. They are doing a job that only a few years before was considered socially useful. They are also providing for their families.

The growth ethos with its nasty side effects is a *social* phenomenon. We all share in it and all have benefited from it. And while some sectors have benefited more than others from the side effects, this fact has only recently come to the fore. What was just, socially useful, and encouraged yesterday becomes today's injustice; and those who quite innocently accepted certain jobs in a market economy that made no attempt to differentiate types of growth suddenly find themselves the victims of changing social attitudes.

Nor can we ignore the suffering that such unemployment would inevitably produce. We cannot simply say that because some have benefited they must now suffer. This is as inhuman as the present tendency to ignore the impact and incidence of social costs.

None of these considerations, however, negates the basic principle that *those who have benefited should be held responsible for the costs they have inflicted.* Rather, they point first to the responsibility of society to assume a portion of the burden, since the benefits have been, at least in part, social. Second, they point again to the necessity for redistribution if any sort of just allocation of costs is to be achieved. Finally, they imply that society has a responsibility to mitigate the suffering resulting from the inclusion of social costs. At a minimum this would entail some kind of income maintenance through any period of transition.

If these guidelines were to be applied, political difficulties would no doubt be encountered. The basic problem is to find a political approach that does at least four things: (1) maintains the principle of responsibility as stated above; (2) effectively and efficiently brings into the cost accounting system the now unpaid social costs; (3) proceeds on the principle that liberty is to be maximized and coercion minimized; and (4) protects the rights and provides for the basic needs of minorities, the poor, and those who are made to suffer. But to state these principles is only the beginning. Like any political issue, the problem of social costs must be hammered out in the arena where competing powers are balanced.

Liberty and Coercion

It is instructive to view the problem of social costs in terms of the polar opposites of liberty and coercion. To deal with it effectively requires a cautious course between the Scylla of catastrophe and the Charybdis of coercion.

Advocates and critics differ markedly in how they assess this dilemma. Many optimistic advocates insist there are no serious problems that we cannot manage through timely applications of technology, substitution of resources, and the flexibility of governments.[11] According to such assessments, it is unnecessary even to consider coercive solutions. Liberty and survival are complementary.

There are good reasons to be skeptical of this optimism. Solutions require a difficult-to-obtain mixture of technical, political, and ethical factors. Those which appeal to voluntary action and conscience seem to be weak on the side of getting the job done. Powerful interest groups have a stake in the continuation of present trends. There is now sufficient reason to believe that simple solutions and laissez-faire attitudes will not be sufficient for dealing with the difficult problems inherent in present patterns of growth. Thus the ethical issue of liberty and coercion is unavoidable in a discussion of the growth debate.

At what point does the threat to survival justify the use of coercion and the abridgment of certain liberties, assuming the failure of appeals to conscience and voluntary action? The more extreme critics unambiguously assert that human survival depends upon coercive control of population, pollution, and depletion. On the other hand, the more extreme advocates assert equally unambiguously that no such action is required. While these extremes are characteristic of only a few on either side, they set the ethical issue in the broadest possible perspective. What they establish is the possibility of a continuum between liberty and coercion along which liberty can be traded off for coercion as problems become demonstrably more severe.[12]

In order to look at this continuum from an ethical perspective several assumptions are necessary. First is the basic ethical assumption that survival (the avoidance of catastrophes) in some way accords with the will of God; that taking steps to ensure the welfare of our grandchildren is morally right. Second is the assumption that the avoidance of catastrophes is the precondition of this welfare and that justice is nearly impossible to establish under extreme threats to survival. Third is the assumption that liberty, like equality, is a regulative principle of justice. It is the relevant norm for social order, as equality is for distribution, and is applied in essentially the same manner. Thus coercion is not desirable unless it can be shown beyond a reasonable doubt with relevant criteria that it is necessary.

By combining these assumptions the following principle is reached: while the most extensive liberty compatible with a like liberty for all is preferable, in the face of widespread loss of life or deterioration in the quality of life, coercion proportionate to the extremity of the situation and democratically decided upon and administered is acceptable. Thus, as the situation becomes demonstrably more grave, a trade-off between liberty and coercion will be required in the absence of voluntary restraints. Roger Shinn sums up the trade-off in the following terms:

> Actually the alternatives are not total freedom or coercion. A spectrum of possibilities is available: uninhibited freedom, rational persuasion, social pressures, economic pressures, manipulative devices, coercion. A society usually settles for something between the extremes. People can live with pressures that leave them room for maneuver.[13]

The problem is to be neither too quick to accept premature coercion—nor in the name of liberty too slow to insist on it when it is necessary in order to prevent widespread suffering. Ideally, of course, solutions would involve liberty as well as survival. But even an approximation of the ideal would presuppose a highly effective political process and a new spirit of cooperation. In the case of social costs where so many interests are involved, many observers do not feel that democracy would be a very efficient or effective instrument. Unfortunately, no ethically acceptable alternative is available. If democratic solutions prove inadequate, then we will be in the tragic dilemma of having to choose between evils. To avoid such a situation, changed attitudes will be essential. Indeed, without a new spirit of cooperation all solutions are in trouble.

Furthermore, we must be wary of two dangers—one obvious, the other not. The obvious danger is paying too much attention to the disguised totalitarians who cry "Wolf" when there is no wolf. The not-so-obvious danger is manipulation that is not quite coercion, particularly when it uses the sophisticated insights of the social sciences. One aspect of this danger is the great reliance that some place on technical solutions to the problem of social costs. The scenario of increasing technological manipulation is abhorrent. According to economist Kenneth Boulding:

> It is a slightly nightmarish thought that social science may be even more damning to mankind than physical science. Physical science merely culminates in the pain and death of the body under the bomb; social science may culminate in the damnation of the soul in the manipulative society.[14]

Jacques Ellul makes this eventuality real in his book *The Technological Society*. While his treatment may be overly deterministic, it does point to an irony in the thought of the advocates who extol the virtues of unrestricted economic growth and look aghast at the mere mention of coercive restrictions. While at the front door they celebrate liberty and resist obvious manipulation and coercion, at the back door they are letting in a more insidious form of the same thing.

To many critics of growth, the present economic system already involves considerable manipulation and coercion. Reliance on technology for solutions offers the potential for even more. We are accustomed to thinking that coercion comes only from governmental sources. But there is no essential difference between coercion overtly emanating from government and coercion covertly imposed by an economic system and a manipulative technology. The former is merely more visible. From an ethical perspective it is desirable to minimize both.

The appeal of the advocates to both liberty and technological solutions is thus not entirely consistent. There must be some way to restrict the economic and technological process. But, in the absence of attitudinal changes, this means there must be a force capable of restricting these processes. Only a social force with legal sanctions can accomplish this. As a result, there is no *a priori* reason why liberty is in any way reduced if an appeal is made to government. Indeed, a case can be made that at present we have external coercion emanating from both government and the economic system, and that these sources are working together to the relative advantage of the few.

What is to be avoided, if possible, is the arbitrary imposition of still more external coercion of whatever form. So in the end, in spite of complexities, the trade-off holds. Steps in trade-off between liberty and coercion are supportable only to the degree required for survival and perhaps a margin for the quality of life. The bias remains in favor of liberty over against coercion in either its covert or overt forms. Coercion in any form is suspect and should only be instituted as a last resort. Programs whose object is to eliminate social costs should at the outset emphasize voluntary action, responsibility, and persuasion, and use a minimum of overt controls. Only when these have demonstrably failed should gradually increasing coercion, democratically agreed upon, be applied.

Chapter 6

IS GROWTH DESIRABLE?

The economic process with its seemingly inherent thrust for growth is many things to many people. To some it is a machine out of control whose primary aim is to exploit the environment and enslave persons. To others it is the *deus ex machina,* for at its base is a godlike creativity which "within reason" can produce anything, solve any problem. Between these views lie still others, some questioning, some fearful, some pessimistic, some realistic, some hopeful. Given this range of opinion, it is difficult to answer the question, Is growth desirable?

One thing is clear, however. Critical decisions with momentous consequences for the future are being forced upon us by our economic activity. The advocates tend to think that these decisions can be delayed or even averted by timely technology tempered only minimally with coercion. Many critics, however, contend that the technological "fix" will not be enough. It is merely oiling the wheels of what is rolling over us. We must make the decisions now, they insist, or we will be subdued and nature will once again have dominion.

Hard, factual information to settle these differing perceptions simply isn't available. The future always holds surprises and consequently permits a wide range of opinions. We have no clear idea what it means to eliminate social costs, nor even which of the many social costs really need to be eliminated. To the advocates it usually means reducing the incidence of the more serious side effects, notably pollution. To all critics it means at least that. To many it means much more. Nothing less than a change in the ideas and values that dominate industrialized culture will satisfy them.

Two Questions

These differing perceptions reveal an extremely important feature of the desirability question. Two problems, not one, are being addressed. The first is the narrower problem of whether the economic process can cleanse itself of the worst social costs as growth continues. The second is the much broader question of whether the thrust for growth and the ideas and values associated with it are desirable. The first is largely a question regarding facts; the second is more ideological.

Earlier we expressed the opinion that the primary issue in the growth debate is the extent to which economic and technical considerations determine values and social policy. If this opinion is correct, then the first of the above problems, though important in itself, is not the crucial one. The central problem is the ideological dispute between those who wish to preserve the present order, in which economic and technological considerations are central, and those who challenge this primacy. In other words, the problem of social costs and the question of the efficacy of the system to cleanse itself are only parts of a much broader ideological struggle. This is not to say that these problems are irrelevant, only that sides taken on them are largely determined by the stand taken on the larger question. The desirability question is being argued much less in the arena of facts than in the arena of values. Advocates and critics talk past each other over the subordinate questions, frequently unaware that a different issue largely determines their positions.

The question, Is the present thrust for growth desirable? is primarily an ethical question. The general positions taken on this question can be outlined as follows:

The Advocates	*The Critics*
1. The economic-technological process is open-ended. It is essentially a human effort to solve problems rationally. It is compatible with most value or belief systems.	1. The economic-technological process is fragmented and specialized with limited objectives. Where accepted, it is usually accompanied by values consistent with its increase and by indifference or hostility to more inclusive values.
2. It solves problems.	2. It has a tendency to create new problems and intensify old ones. It diverts attention away from nontechnical social problems. Its success, viewed narrowly, is predetermined because only those problems are selected which

have potential solutions. Success is judged on the basis of criteria derived from the process.

3. It is a necessary means to economic and social improvement. It is only a part of the social-cultural process.

3. It is a means become an end and involves repression and alienation. At times it even gives the appearance of an autonomous force. It is the dominant factor in the social-cultural process. While providing material improvements, it neglects the totality of the human experience.

4. It is value free and controlled by social choice.

4. It has its own ideology and values which, like most ideologies, are unrecognized by those who hold them. It forces choices and is directed, even if not always controlled, by a large economic-technological elite.

5. It is the primary force overcoming the vagaries of nature.

5. It involves the exploitation of nature and the destruction of ecological support systems.

6. Its continuation is vital for the solution of present and future problems.

6. Reliance on it for the solution of problems will lead to further environmental deterioration. Problems as well as solutions are not only technical but political, ethical, and attitudinal.

7. It is basically a sound process. Social cost problems have only recently been perceived and will be effectively dealt with as soon as society puts its mind to finding technical solutions. What is needed is more, not less, technology.

7. It is a basically sound but limited process. Above all, it needs to be subordinated to independent value criteria. Social costs have not previously been recognized, largely because of the ideology that has accompanied the process.

8. It benefits all—including the poor, through the "trickle down" effect.

8. Its benefits and costs are maldistributed. The thrust behind it has been a cause of the neglect of the poor.

9. Its direction can be altered by rational human beings acting with only a minimum of government intervention.

9. Its direction can be altered only by a new ethical and political consciousness.

10. Attacks on the process are untimely. If successful, they will block the process when it is most needed.

10. Attacks are necessary in order to get at the problems at hand.

The Critics' Biases

To charge an opponent with biased or ideological thinking is an old debater's trick. It wins no points in this case, but rival values are very much at issue and problems of bias quite important. Already we have explored the critics' charge that growth is an ideology of technical power. To round out this discussion we must turn the spotlight back on the critics and consider their biases.

Not unexpectedly the advocates focus countercriticism

on the relative affluence, elitism, and whiteness of the critics of growth. In the words of Anthony Crosland:

> Their approach is hostile to growth in principle and indifferent to the needs of ordinary people. It has a manifest class bias, and reflects a set of middle and upper class value judgments. Its champions are often kindly and dedicated people. But they are affluent and fundamentally, though of course not consciously, they want to kick the ladder down behind them.[1]

To this way of thinking the current emphasis on such problems as ecology and the costs of growth represents a "cop-out" or diversion away from the real problems of racism, war, urban problems, and poverty. It is an attempt to focus on pseudo problems in order to avoid issues which, if faced, would threaten the critics' elitist position.

For poor minority groups in America the emphasis on ecology and the costs of growth seems to come at a time when they are on the verge of securing a larger piece of the economic pie. Or, failing that, growth can at least measurably improve general material conditions. To these groups, growth criticism appears to be a conscious effort to close off future economic opportunity, to force the minorities to remain in an inferior economic status.

Lutheran pastor Richard Neuhaus adds two other charges: antihumanism and totalitarianism. For Neuhaus, appeals that emphasize nature and the need to conform to ecosystems represent a new form of nature determinism. The gods of nature are being resuscitated in subtle ways and the needs of persons are being sacrificed to them.

In regard to totalitarianism, Neuhaus points to the

frequent appeals to "survival" in the literature of the critics. Specifically, he points to the ease with which critics such as Garrett Hardin and Paul Ehrlich appeal to coercion to ensure survival. Neuhaus does not feel that an environmental crisis of "survival" proportions is imminent. Therefore he sees this emphasis on survival as naïve politically. It reveals a totalitarian approach to social structure and suggests an ideological rigidity and political centralism foreign to democratic traditions. Moreover, it is deceptively elitist.

> America has had some bad visions and some good ones, some bad dreams and some good dreams. "Survival" is a bad dream. . . . When survival is king, all questions of right and wrong are irrelevant and diversionary. The question is not whether this measure or that is right or wrong: it is necessary. The word "necessary" is emblazoned on the pendants of every totalitarian force that has plagued our tortured human history. . . . Whenever the rich exploit the poor and the strong oppress the weak, they have pleaded the law of necessity. There is no atrocity or indifference to suffering that has not been covered by the law of necessity, the law of survival. And always there is a small clique redefining and reinforcing the threat, and prescribing the measures necessary to survive it. Today a group of cackling witches report dire events foretold in their ecological caldron and bid to become our new National-Security Managers.[2]

Finally, the countercriticism points to the social implications of slowing growth. The poor and blue-collar classes would be the first victims of efforts to clean up the environment through higher prices and lost jobs. The advocates point to the critics' frequent failure to deal with this and other social consequences of their programs. The charge follows that at best the critics are insensitive and at worst they are consciously using ecology and the costs of growth to protect their own relative affluence.

This countercriticism is partially justified and must be dealt with by those who criticize economic and technological growth. Some of the critics rather neatly fit the stereotype. They tend to neglect structural and institutional questions and to overlook the value of a functioning economy. They frequently fail to investigate the larger implications of their criticisms. They often seem to focus on single issues and to neglect social-ethical issues of long-standing importance. For some there seems to be a desire to return to nature and to avoid the pressures of a technological culture. Others, notably British economist Ezra Mishan, at times appear to want a return to a less harried era before industrialization, to an imagined "golden age" before traffic congestion and crowded public facilities. Finally, almost all critics attack abundance, frequently forgetting that abundance is an advantage enjoyed by only a few of the world's people. All these weaknesses, especially when pooled and attributed to all critics irrespective of differences, add considerable weight to the countercriticism.

The Problems Remain

Out of all this, one thing is clear: unless critics include in their criticism of growth some provision for a more equitable distribution of benefits and burdens, and unless they include more attention to the interrelation of other critical social problems, they are justly to be condemned for pushing an upper-class ideology. Without these added elements their programs freeze existing income and wealth differentials and push the burden of paying social costs more heavily on the poor.

This does not mean, however, that the countercriticism is completely justified. The problems remain, no matter what biases are brought to them. All critics are not equally vulnerable to this counterattack. There is a strong ethical emphasis in what many of them have to say, and established ways of thinking deserve radical challenge at many points.

Considering the diversity of the critical position, the countercriticism is certain to hit some mark. What is striking is not the partial validity of the counterattacks, but the frequency with which the radical implications of growth criticism are overlooked. The position of the critics strikes at the very heart of present economic relationships in which the environment *is* neglected and, more importantly, persons *are* exploited. The human costs of the growth process alone are enormous.

Barry Commoner is an example of a critic who is also sensitive to the issues of social justice. Commoner, like many other critics, maintains that

> the root cause of the crisis is not to be found in how men interact with nature, but in how they interact with each other—that to solve the environmental crisis we must solve the problems of poverty, racial injustice and war; that the debt to nature which is the measure of the environmental crisis cannot be paid, person by person, in recycled bottles or ecologically sound habits, but in the ancient coin of social justice; that, in sum, a peace among men must precede the peace with nature. . . .
>
> There appears to be no middle ground; if, as we must, we are to solve the environmental crisis, we will need to choose between two paths—one leading toward a more just distri-

bution of the nation's resources and wealth, and the other toward further intensification of the present unequal and—in my view—unjust distribution of wealth.[3]

For those like Richard Neuhaus who combine a concern for the poor with negative judgments on the critics of growth, there is a particular tragedy. Their stance, when coupled with the equally tragic stance of critics who ignore the poor, makes enemies of potential allies. When poverty and environmental expenditures are both relatively small, critics and countercritics are like children arguing over crumbs while the cake is being eaten by a common foe. Internecine warfare is not necessary, in spite of the partially valid criticisms that can be made of both sides. What is called for is an alliance on the basis of a common critique of current economic patterns. Again in the words of Barry Commoner:

> We can approach the truth about the environmental crisis, and learn what we must do to survive it, only by seeking out its origins, linking these with the economic and social processes that govern how we live in the world, and by learning how to change these processes so that they conform with the needs of the environment and of the people who inhabit it.[4]

In spite of widely differing social positions, the basis for an alliance exists. From the perspective of Christian ethics such an alliance is essential. There will be little advance on either poverty or social costs without a combined effort, for otherwise energy will be dissipated. A divided opposition in the face of a united opponent is bad politics as well as bad ethics.

The major responsibility for seeking such an alliance

rests with the critics. They have more room for maneuver and cannot ethically ignore the long-standing issues of poverty, racism, and war. They must avoid becoming the captives of one issue. They must press home the implications of their critique as these apply to other long-standing ethical issues, and they must seek solutions to the social cost problems, solutions that do not preserve or worsen inequities. Otherwise their criticism, however factually sound, will be ethically and politically suspect.

In their own defense the critics point out how much of the countercriticism could as effectively be directed to the advocates' position. It too tends to "cop out" on significant social issues. It too gets its most effective support from the affluent. It too—perhaps to an even greater degree—depends on an elite. It too can be antihumanist. In fact, about the only criticism that does not seem to apply is the charge of inviting totalitarianism, but even this is a matter of degree. The present economic and technological world view, as we have seen, is not without totalitarian implications in spite of its appeal to liberty. Economic bondage is no less oppressive for being disguised.

Nor can we overlook the seriousness of social costs whether or not the critics are trying "to kick the ladder down behind them." As bearers of bad news the critics are counterattacked. Nevertheless, weakening their influence will not get rid of the problems. They are quite serious and not very respectful of ideological boundaries.

Recognizing that the debate is highly ideological, what can we say about desirability? What should the role of the economic process be in eliminating social costs? And finally, what are the possibilities of changing present directions?

Neither All Nor Nothing

Without adopting an ethic of the happy medium, we can observe that all-or-nothing judgments do not seem to fit. Science, technology, and economic analysis are crucial to solving many problems, maintaining a decent standard of living, and increasing material standards in developing countries. To throw them out would be foolish even if it were possible. The scientist, the engineer, and the economist all have vital roles to play. Furthermore, a failure of nerve or a turn toward escapist ideologies would inevitably have disastrous consequences at all levels of social organization. It is not always possible to preserve what is good in an established world view once it is undermined. There is a tendency in rejecting one view to move to a polar opposite, "throwing out the baby with the bath water." This we cannot afford.

Yet to give the process free rein to continue as it is will mean the continued primacy of a narrow range of values, possible environmental collapse, and the maintenance of present forms of repression. It will also perpetuate the present tendency to emphasize "things" over persons, the material over the spiritual, means over ends.

If the only alternatives are the present thrust for growth or its rejection in favor of a pristine past, a judgment on desirability is meaningless. From a Christian ethical perspective neither is desirable. Instead of these dead-end alternatives we should seek scientific, technical, and economic solutions that conform to our twin criteria of environmental soundness and contribution to human welfare. This means encouraging the scientist, the engineer, and the economist; but also placing their activities under a changed value system. Such a judgment is closer to the critical position in the debate, though it tries to pull together the best of both sides. It is also easier to state than to realize. We should have no illusions about realizing the best of two worlds immediately.

There are reasons, however, to be cautiously optimistic about a change in consciousness. While there may be no immediate resolution of the contrasting views of advocates and critics, in the longer run, world views are open to change. The problem of social costs has a factual element, and world views are susceptible to change when new "facts" come into the picture. Still, world views are notoriously resistant to change. New "facts" can be declared irrelevant, interpreted away, or rejected as inaccurate. But if the gap is so wide that no forced consistency is possible, value conflict is inevitable and one precondition of change is established. The problem of social costs may be one such gap-producing phenomenon.

Equally important, world views are not entirely self-enclosed or subjective. In industrialized societies of the West, competing ideologies hold certain norms in common—love, justice, and equality, for example. And while the ideological application of these norms is usually more important than the formal norms themselves, these common values do have independent content that can be appealed to in support of a changed direction. What is more, they serve as limits to what is morally acceptable.

Cautious optimism is also possible because of the survival in Western culture of values that are not dependent on the economic process. These alternative values can be and are being appealed to in criticism of the thrust for growth. The economic process has not produced an all-encompassing cultural synthesis. Nor has it satisfied some very important human needs, notably privacy, spirituality, and deep personal relationships.

Moreover, political conflict—the balancing of power against power—has already had some effect in altering the direction of the process. It is difficult to assess the impact of this political pressure, but legislatures are passing new environmental laws. Old laws are being enforced for the first time. Small but well-organized groups continue to be successful in selected battles against the worst offenders. Environmental bond issues pass with relative ease. These successes may be only initial skirmishes with the main battle yet to be fought. Nevertheless, there seems to be a growing awareness even among many of the advocates that significant steps need to be taken.

But what will happen if and when the correction of social costs leads to higher prices, higher taxes, lower profits, and lower rates of growth—all distinct possibilities? At a minimum, increased resistance can be expected. It is one thing on behalf of a social good to suffer lower profits or to pay slightly higher prices and taxes for a while. But when institutional survival and a whole style of life are threatened, a new dimension is added. We need only look at the events following the Arab oil embargo in 1973 and the economic recession of 1974–1975 to see how quickly environmental concerns can be jettisoned in favor of maintaining the "standard of living" and full employment.

Thus we must emphasize the word "cautious" and point to the real danger, which is not economic nihilism but the perpetuation of an unchecked thrust for growth. Growth is here to stay for the immediate future. Indeed, it can solve or help to solve many important problems. Yet, to rely on growth, or on any means that are based primarily on material considerations, is clearly insufficient. Manipulation of economic and technological means alone will not get at the political, ethical, and religious dimensions of the social cost problem. For these a changed world view is absolutely essential, since economic and technical manipulations deal primarily with things.

Herein, however, lies the real dilemma. While ideas (world views) do affect material relationships, it is equally true that material relationships affect ideas. In Western culture the ideas, values, and meanings reflecting a material base of economic growth dominate. Karl Marx, who held that the material dominates the ideal, seems correct in this instance. To carry the Marxist analysis a step further, there may be little chance to change this situation without a change in the basic material relationships.

The current dominance of the material over the ideal in determining the basic direction of industrialized countries is firmly rooted. Powerful forces are entrenched on the side of preserving this dominance and resisting all challenges by alternative world views. Moral exhortation is unlikely to be effective. Political confrontation is easily muted by words and superficial corrections. Thus it is not likely that any world view will alter the present pattern of dominance in any meaningful way without the material conditions themselves changing.

What is the possibility of change in the material

conditions? To be sure, no one really knows. The case may be, however, that the problems of depletion and pollution are so severe that present material relationships will of necessity change. The open question is whether the present economic process can be effectively manipulated to avert depletion and pollution crises. If it can, then the present relationships probably will hold and only those social costs involving physical survival will be eliminated. If it cannot, then the equilibrium economy to be discussed in the next chapters will be the primary alternative. In this case the material relationships will necessarily change and create a situation where it *may* be possible to bring more encompassing values into the mix.

Nevertheless, pollution and depletion limits are some way off. In the meantime the task is, at minimum, to prepare the ethical, religious, and political foundations so that alternatives are available to avert wholesale social and cultural breakdown as limits are approached. Moral exhortation, political confrontation, consciousness raising, continuation of the attack on social problems, and scientific-ethical dialogues are all essential. Not only might such efforts exert an influence on present patterns, but the future is open and the Spirit works in strange ways. There is hope for a better future.

Yes and No to Growth

To sum up then, we can say that the theoretical case for growth is strong. In practice, of course, it falls short, far short, when we consider the moral idealism reflected in some of the theory. Moreover, the arguments for growth are used ideologically to further the position of those who benefit most from growth. Yet these negative considerations are not alone sufficient to declare growth undesirable.

Far more damaging to the case for continued growth is the incidence of social costs. Here, however, there is much confusion as to what constitutes significant social costs, as well as an alarming lack of hard information. To say with many critics that the costs of growth now exceed the benefits is simply not evident, at least not conclusively enough to persuade the majority of Americans. Actually, there is no way at this time to determine whether the costs exceed the benefits. This is a subjective value judgment.

The growth process admittedly has many undesirable aspects. But this does not automatically allow us to infer that growth should cease. Rather, it points to the task of eliminating the undesirable and preserving the desirable elements. It is a call for a differentiated or selective growth policy to replace the present policy of undifferentiated growth. We need to pursue a type of growth that is environmentally sound, within the long-range carrying capacity of the earth, controlled by values not themselves products of the economic process, and distributed more equitably than at present.

We have dealt at some length with the question, Is growth desirable? It has been our purpose to bring attention to social costs, to point to the neglected ethical elements in the debate, and to call for a change in the current structure and consciousness of growth. Industrial societies have made economic growth a primary social goal. In so doing they have unleashed a powerful process with little regard for its negative consequences and long-range implications.

The question of desirability is thus preeminently a question about who we are and how we want to live. Should our society be determined by economic and technological modes and values? Or should it be a society in which the economic process is a means subordinated to the higher ends—e.g., responsible stewardship, the needs of people and nature, and, ultimately, God's justice and love? The answer is clearly the latter. Growth yes, but not as it is presently constructed and given such a dominant position. Growth yes, but differentiated growth.

The growth process has a momentum, the direction of which will be difficult to alter, much less reverse. It is well buttressed by sound, by unsound but appealing, and by purely ideological arguments. In the absence of physical limitations it will in all likelihood continue in its present direction without major change, at least into the foreseeable future. No doubt some corrections will be made and some of the social costs eliminated. But these corrections will have the likely effect of strengthening, not reducing, the thrust and of preserving the social and cultural dominance of economic and technological considerations.

However, if the futurists are correct in asserting that limits to growth exist, then a clash is coming. The clash will be between those who desire ever more growth and those who see the limits and desire a differentiated growth process. Even more, it will be a clash between the thrust and the limits themselves, a clash with potentially more devastating consequences. But the thrust may be so strong that we will refuse or be unable to see approaching limits. And what can be expected when an entire world view is threatened; when a society and culture built on

given economic relationships must change those relationships? What are the long-range implications of a differentiated growth policy? Perhaps the futurists can give
us a few clues.

Chapter 7

THE LIMITS
TO GROWTH

Desirable or not, insist the futurists, present patterns of undifferentiated growth cannot continue. The debate between critics and advocates has been too narrow, too shortsighted. The problems of population, food, pollution, energy, and resource depletion are interrelated and have long-range implications of staggering proportions. Immediate cooperative action on a worldwide scale alone will avert serious breakdown due to nature-imposed limits to growth. The action demanded within industrialized nations is a change in economic structure and social consciousness of mammoth proportions, in magnitude not unlike the shift from a feudal to an industrial economy. The crisis facing industrial civilization with its dynamic thrust for growth is far greater than even the critics imagine. We must shift from an economy of undifferentiated growth to one that is in balance with the total environment. In the words of "A Blueprint for Survival":

> The principal defect of the industrial way of life with its ethos of expansion is that it is not sustainable. Its termina-

tion within the lifetime of someone born today is inevitable
—unless it continues to be sustained for a while longer by
an entrenched minority at the cost of imposing great suffering on the rest of mankind. We can be certain, however,
that sooner or later it will end (only the precise time
and circumstances are in doubt), and that it will do so in
one of two ways: either against our will, in a succession of
famines, epidemics, social crises and wars; or because
we want it to—because we wish to create a society which
will not impose hardship and cruelty upon our children—
in a succession of thoughtful, humane, and measured
changes.[1]

The futurists have only a vague notion of how an
economy in balance with the total environment would
operate. They cannot even agree on what to call it.
Several names have been suggested, none of which is
entirely satisfactory. The term "equilibrium economy" is
perhaps the best overall, though it suggests a lack of
dynamism that need not characterize the economy. The
image "spaceship earth," popularized by Barbara Ward
and Kenneth Boulding, offers the most complete picture
but is seldom encountered in discussions.

The projections of the futurists are not wholly new. In
the nineteenth century, Thomas Malthus, David Ricardo,
and John Stuart Mill made roughly similar projections.
For over a century now these projections have been
ignored. Their reassertion in the early 1970's under
changed circumstances and with greater sophistication
has the appearance of novelty. Nevertheless, the futurists
in essence have reopened an old debate. The same
arguments used to rebut Malthus, Ricardo, and Mill are
now being turned against the futurists. The difference,
however, is that the world view of growth, which made

this rebuttal convincing, is itself now under attack. As a consequence, the old debate has new vitality.

The Limits-to-Growth Thesis

The possibility of ultimate limits to economic growth, especially to those aspects of growth which pollute and deplete, has been raised before by some of the critics. For example, the conservation movement early in this century was concerned with the depletion of natural resources. Kenneth Boulding introduced the "spaceship" imagery in the 1960's. Barry Commoner has made it clear there are limits to possible interference with ecosystems.[2]

Nevertheless, little of this speculation was ever developed systematically or the consequences delineated forcefully. In 1971, Jay W. Forrester, professor of management at the Massachusetts Institute of Technology (M.I.T.) and a computer specialist, published the initial findings of a team effort that used a computer model developed by Forrester himself.[3] This initial report was subsequently followed in 1972 by a slightly updated and more popularly written report by other team members under the leadership of Dennis Meadows and the sponsorship of the Club of Rome.[4] In late 1974 appeared the report of still another computer study, also under the auspices of the Club of Rome, but not connected with the work done at M.I.T.[5] These studies bring the issues into sharp focus. In particular the controversial Meadows led report, The Limits to Growth, requires our scrutiny because, rightly or wrongly, it states the futurists' position most forcefully and has attracted by far the most attention.

What the M.I.T. team has done is to use the computer model developed by Forrester—called "system dynamics"—to explore the dynamic behavior of five interrelated and exponentially growing variables: depletion of natural resources, demand for food, pollution, capital investment, and population. It is essential to keep in mind that the model and hence the results rest on certain assumptions that were a product of available data and the team's own value judgments. The computer's sole function was to trace dynamic behavior once the assumptions were programmed. Therefore, the results are conditioned by the validity of the assumptions, the accuracy of the data, and the acceptability of the value judgments.

The M.I.T. team made a special effort to detail its assumptions, for they are the element of greatest vulnerability. Clearly the most important assumptions have to do with the nature of exponential growth within a finite environment. According to the reports, all key variables grow exponentially. The earth, upon which this growth depends, is finite. Therefore, there are limits to the growth of the variables.

To clarify this assumption we must first look at the nature of exponential growth. Any quantity that steadily increases by a constant percentage of the whole over a given period is said to grow exponentially. Savings accounts that draw compound interest are an example of such growth. Exponential growth can be both misleading and treacherous since a variable can be growing (for example, GNP at roughly 3 percent per year, with a doubling time of 23 years) for long periods without reaching significant size. Then, within one or two doubling periods, its size becomes overwhelming. As a simple illustration we could take a chessboard and put one grain of rice in a corner square, then two grains in the next square, four in the next, and so on down the line, doubling the number each time. Long before the last square is reached we would be buried in rice. This can also be illustrated graphically.

Exponential Growth, Doubling Times and Limits

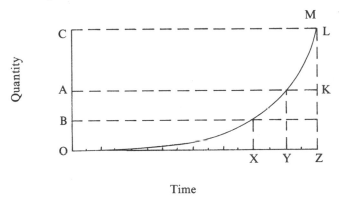

Exponential growth curves look much like the curve OM in the graph. For long periods of time increases are nearly imperceptible, as in the first few squares on the chessboard. Then in a short time (period XY) the quantity doubles from OB to OA. Now if quantity OA is a physical limit (represented by line AK) above which the variable cannot grow, this means that growth from half the limit to the limit occurs in a relatively short period. This is the treachery of the curve. At half the limit there may be no signs that a limit is in sight and being approached. Then in a very short period severe adjustments may be necessary to accommodate the fact that a limit has been reached. The adjustments may not be pleasant. For example, if the growth in question happens to be that of population, the adjustment may be in the form of widespread starvation as the limit is approached.

Limit AK, however, may only be a temporary limit dictated by price or the state of the arts. If through some technical innovation, resource substitution, or new discovery the limit is pushed up to CL, the result changes, but not significantly. At best this pushing up of a limit will only mean a period of grace (YZ) before a new limit is reached. This is important for those who claim, for example, that resource depletion is not a serious problem. Doubling or even quadrupling available resources will not greatly change the situation. Quadrupling the quantity of resources will yield about 45 years at a consumption rate of 3 percent. Then a new limit is reached, and scarcity will be encountered unless, of course, the limit itself is pushed up indefinitely. A further critical assumption of the reports is that limits cannot be pushed up indefinitely, or even much more, by technical developments.

In one way or another, all five variables considered by the M.I.T. team relate to the two primary problems of population and economic growth. The critical limits that make the increases of population and material output problematic are the capacity of the world to produce food, absorb pollution, and yield natural resources. *The Limits to Growth* explores each of these in succession. In each case it arrives at the conclusion that limits do in fact exist and that there is no possible way to avoid them short of radically changing our growth patterns. A closer look at the second and third limits, capacity to absorb pollution and availability of natural resources, highlights several critical assumptions of the reports in regard to economic growth.

In considering natural resource limits, the team first gathered available data on a wide range of resources, largely relying on statistics from the U.S. Bureau of Mines. Five calculations were then made.

1. Known global reserves.
2. The number of years these reserves will last at present consumption rates.
3. Projected growth rates of consumption.
4. The number of years reserves will last at the projected rates of consumption.
5. The number of years reserves will last at the projected rates of consumption, allowing for a fivefold increase in resources.

These calculations provided the resource data for the computer model. The last calculation of a fivefold increase in resources was by far the most significant. It assumed that a fivefold increase would represent something of an outer limit to potentially available resources. What this apparently liberal assumption is saying, however, is that technical innovation, substitution, and new resource discoveries together can produce *no more* than a fivefold increase in aggregate resources. Although this multiple of five, rather arbitrarily selected by the team, has no empirical significance, it points to the most important assumption: while consumption will increase exponentially, the combination of factors pushing back resource limits will not.

The team admits that simple calculations of resource reserves and consumption rates are not sufficient. Nonrenewable resource availability in fact depends on varying grades of ore, production costs, new mining technology, elasticity of demand, and substitution.[6] The team attempted to include these factors in the feedback loops of the computer model. Even so, the general results of the study were determined much more by the assumption of exponentially growing demand running into a limited supply. *The Limits to Growth* concludes:

> As demand continues to increase . . . the advance of technology is not fast enough to counteract the rising costs of discovery, extraction, processing, and distribution. Price begins to rise, slowly at first and then very rapidly. . . .
>
> The earth's crust contains vast amounts of these raw materials which man has learned to mine and to transform into useful things. However vast these amounts may be, they are not infinite. Now that we have seen how suddenly an exponentially growing quantity approaches a fixed upper limit, the following statement should not come as a surprise. *Given present resource consumption rates and the projected increase in these rates, the great majority of the currently important nonrenewable resources will be extremely costly 100 years from now.* The above statement remains true regardless of the most optimistic assumptions about undiscovered reserves, technological advances, substitution, or recycling, as long as the demand for resources continues to grow exponentially.[7]

Similar conclusions were reached regarding pollution. Here, however, the team was more restrained. They discovered that the available data are hardly sufficient for conclusive judgments. Nevertheless, the reports assume that pollution is increasing exponentially, that limits exist to the capacity of the world to absorb it, and that technological innovations can produce no better than a fourfold reduction of pollution generation from all sources. In particular, they emphasize the threat of thermal pollution. Generally, however, the reports are more optimistic on the possibility that the technological process can solve many specific pollution problems. Yet *The Limits to Growth* insists that present patterns cannot continue.

> We do not know the precise upper limit of the earth's ability to absorb any single kind of pollution, much less its ability to absorb the combination of all kinds of pollution. We do know however that there *is* an upper limit. It has already been surpassed in many local environments. The surest way to reach the upper limit globally is to increase exponentially both the number of people and the polluting activities of each person.[8]

The team did not use a computer in making all these assumptions. The uniqueness of these M.I.T. reports does not lie in the assumptions, which are generally shared with other futurists, but in the attempt to model and program the assumptions, the available data, and the interrelations of the variables. The details of the model and the computer program are beyond our scope. The results of the computer runs, however, were significant in several instances.

The most significant result was the repeated overshoot of limits and collapse. The variables would all grow for a time, even when the team's most liberal assumptions were applied, overshoot limits, and then decrease precipitously. From this repeated behavior of the model *The Limits to Growth* concludes: "We can thus say with some confidence that, under the assumption of no major change in the present system, population and industrial growth will certainly stop within the next century." [9]

This pattern of overshoot and collapse was characteristic no matter which limit was reached first. The team considered each limit in turn by artificially decreasing the growth rates of the factors corresponding to it. In each case, growth eventually leveled off and rapidly declined as a new limit came to dominate the system. In the case of population, this has rather obvious implications.

Forrester, in particular, stresses the successive nature of the limits.

> One can argue that exhaustion of natural resources is not the most likely limitation on population growth. Actual stocks of natural resources may be greater than . . . has been assumed here. . . .
>
> If natural resources do not limit population growth and slow the pace of industrialization, however, some other force in the world system will eventually do so. . . .
>
> A point may be reached where continuing the industrial process means a population collapse from pollution, while stopping the industrial process means a population collapse from failure of the technical support systems of the society. . . .
>
> When one pressure or difficulty is alleviated, the result may be merely to substitute a new problem for the old. In particular, the industrialized societies have come to depend on technology to solve their problems. This succeeded when technology was improving so rapidly that it could exploit geographical space and natural resources faster than popula-

tion could increase. But now, as technology reaches the point of diminished returns and begins to run short on space and resources, the technological "solution" may more and more be only the substitution of one crisis for another.[10]

The results of the study should not be given undue authority. They are only as valid as the original assumptions and the accuracy of the data. The computer is an advance over intuitive projections primarily in its ability to keep straight the web of feedback loops linking the five variables.

The M.I.T. team is aware of the many limitations of the study. *The Limits to Growth* is punctuated with reservations and warnings. The team continually insists that the reports represent a preliminary effort. They are aware of a lack of empirical data on which conclusions can be firmly grounded. They make clear that the model is only a projection of current patterns and not a prediction of the inevitable. They are straightforward in presenting their assumptions and asking for criticism. Finally, they admit that there are technical problems of aggregation, of delineating the precise interrelationships between variables, and of computer sensitivity to small changes.

For all this, the reports are still valuable—not only because few comparable studies exist but also because they seem accurate enough to raise grave doubts about the current pattern of economic growth. The results of the study therefore warrant serious consideration and further development.

One significant development has been the second report from the Club of Rome, *Mankind at the Turning Point,* which summarizes the main points of another computer project under Mihajlo Mesarovic and Eduard Pestel. This project developed independently of the M.I.T. study but benefited from many criticisms directed at the Forrester-Meadows approach. The project culminated in a large conference of scientists in Austria in the spring of 1974.

Generally the Mesarovic-Pestel work is more optimistic than the M.I.T. reports. Without downplaying the interrelated crises, it uses a minimum of doomsday rhetoric, preferring to emphasize the possibilities.

Our scientifically conducted analysis of the long-term world development based on all available data points out quite clearly that [the present] course leads to disaster. It is most urgent that we do not avert our eyes from the dangers ahead, but face the challenge squarely and assess alternative paths of development in a positive and hopeful spirit.[11]

Like the M.I.T. study, it looks at the converging problems from a global perspective. But in a significant departure it divides the world into ten regions. To view the world homogeneously, as in the M.I.T. study, is inaccurate and misleading, according to Mesarovic and Pestel. Obviously, different parts of the world face different problems. Population growth and food shortages are far greater problems in India than in the United States. Conversely, pollution and depletion of resources are far worse in the United States. The Arab countries have quite different problems and prospects than those of Western Europe. A regional approach to global problems is superior because it accounts for these and other differences and can offer specific plans for each region. With the Forrester-Meadows approach we are left with only the insistence that undifferentiated growth must cease and with no specific direction for obviously dissimilar regions. Yes, on a global scale undifferentiated growth must cease, agree Mesarovic and Pestel, but this may mean quite different policies in different regions.

This regional approach in combination with the gravity of the problems leads Mesarovic and Pestel to stress worldwide cooperation and immediate action. Their computer runs time and again reveal: (1) that global problems can only be solved through the cooperation of the ten regions; (2) that the pursuit by any one region of immediate gains at the expense of other regions is ruinous to *all* in the long run; (3) that time delays invariably make solutions more difficult and more expensive.

Three insights of immediate ethical interest emerge from these reports. All three present a challenge to conventional wisdom, revealing that time-honored ways of improving the human condition may no longer work.

The first of these is the interrelatedness of problems. What we face is not a population crisis and an economic crisis, independent of each other, but a common crisis involving both population and economic growth. The various elements feed back on each other, a fact that above all renders reductionist solutions tenuous. Exclusive efforts to relieve one set of symptoms only means that another set associated with another limit becomes critical. Thus, if through a variety of technological innovations strides are made in removing pollution symptoms, crowding becomes more severe, resources are further depleted, or a food shortage threatens. Only solutions that deal simultaneously with the five variables will be sufficient. Piecemeal efforts simply will not work.[12] And this forces us once again to realize that workable solutions inevitably have technical, political, and ethical dimensions, none of which can be ignored.

Closely related is a second insight concerning unilateral action by any one region. The pursuit of immediate self-interest, however beneficial in the short run, will ultimately harm not only other regions but eventually even the self-interested region. Besides implying conventional wisdom about world cooperation, this insight has several potentially disturbing implications. It may mean that the pursuit of growth by any one region to alleviate unemployment or maintain standards of living is no longer a viable option. It may also mean that the less developed regions may never reach the material levels of the more developed regions. Actually—as some Third World spokesmen are already saying—the less developed regions may be in a better position to survive pollution and depletion crises; and in order to prevent vulnerability they should pursue other goals than economic growth. This unavoidably raises the distribution issue and calls into question the inordinate consumption of resources by the United States. Now, not only are Americans convicted ethically for consuming more than their share, but their consumption may also be paving the way for their own ruin. The world has become an interdependent whole. No longer will unilateral decisions on growth, resource consumption, or war suffice. Only cooperative action taking into account a multitude of variables will avert serious crises.

The third insight concerns the future. Attempts to produce improvements in the short run may make matters worse in the long run; and conversely, efforts to make the long range viable may initially cause hardships. This raises ethical conundrums of considerable proportion. For example, if it is decided to feed the hungry now, a rather obvious ethical choice on the face of it, more people may live only to cause greater suffering and death in a later crisis. On the other hand, if efforts to curb economic growth are taken in the name of long-range equilibrium, unemployment and economic depression may be the immediate result.

Criticism of the Limits Reports

The M.I.T. study in particular has met with determined opposition and criticism. This should come as no surprise considering the ideological aspects of the growth debate. A good deal of criticism, especially from the advocates of growth, has been virulent. The team has been accused of insensitivity to the needs of the poor and of fundamental economic and technological ignorance. Economist Carl Kaysen dubs his critique "The Computer That Printed Out Wolf." [13] Scientist Martin Shubik characterizes the study as simplistic, superficial, and of virtually no behavioral-scientific content. [14] The tone of this criticism is perhaps best caught by economists Peter Passell and Marc Roberts and lawyer Leonard Ross:

"The Limits to Growth," in our view, is an empty and misleading work. Its imposing apparatus of computer technology and systems jargon conceals a kind of intellectual

Rube Goldberg device—one which makes arbitrary assumptions, shakes them up and comes out with arbitrary conclusions that have the ring of science. "Limits" pretends to a degree of certainty so exaggerated as to obscure the few modest (and unoriginal) insights that it genuinely contains. Less than pseudoscience and little more than polemical fiction, "The Limits to Growth" is best summarized not as a rediscovery of the laws of nature but as a rediscovery of the oldest maxim of computer science: Garbage In, Garbage Out.[15]

It is not necessary to react with such fire to see the shortcomings of the reports. Indeed, most of the criticisms have been anticipated by the M.I.T. team. Some have been accepted as true so far as they go; others have been rejected. None, however, has shaken the confidence of the team in regard to the basic conclusions.

Many of the criticisms are technical and beyond our present scope.[16] Nonetheless one stands out and demands our full attention. The M.I.T. team fails, according to many advocates of growth, adequately to take into account the ability of new technologies to increase the food supply, to "create" new resources, and eventually to provide a nonpolluting production process. That this objection is at the heart of the criticism is not surprising. It is the debate over the technological "fix" and ultimately over the desirability of economic growth all over again.

The M.I.T. study comes down squarely in the center of the ideological debate over desirability despite its seeming preoccupation with the question of possibility. There is simply not enough empirical evidence on *either* side to make a convincing case for or against the possibility of avoiding limits. To say this does *not* mean there is *no* empirical evidence. There is certainly enough evidence to conclude, for example, that the exponential growth of population cannot continue much longer. We could also cite the empirical evidence on pollution levels and the effects of pollution on ecosystems and human health. Nor does this rule out the possibility that we will be able to decide the issue of limits on the basis of empirical evidence in the not-too-distant future. Rather it is to say that assessments of whether the M.I.T. study has satisfactorily taken account of technology and substitution rest to a large degree on ideological and even metaphysical judgments. Indeed, there is a remarkable correlation of views on the questions of desirability and possibility. Generally, those who favor the current pattern of technological growth reject the M.I.T. study. Conversely, those who wish to see restrictions placed on the technological process celebrate the conclusions of the study. In other words, *the question of possibility is seemingly being determined by the question of desirability.*

The central criticism is stated in various ways. Boiled down, however, it amounts to Carl Kaysen's assertion that "the advance of technology, like the growth of population and industry, has also been proceeding exponentially." Kaysen concludes:

Once an exponentially improving technology is admitted into the model, along with exponentially growing population and production, the nature of its outcomes changes sharply. The inevitability of crisis when a limit is reached disappears, since the "limits" themselves are no longer fixed, but growing exponentially too. The qualitative character of the results then depends on the fine details of the model, and, in particular, on the differences between the growth rates of the most important variables. Catastrophes need no longer be the rule, and more stable outcomes, in particular continuing growth at lower rates, now become possible.[17]

According to this view, the team's assumptions of a fivefold increase in resources and a fourfold reduction in pollution from all sources are unrealistic. The team's liberal limits are far too pessimistic. The outcome of the computer runs is determined by these assumptions. As the old proverb has it, "what is shouted into the forest, the forest echoes back." It takes no computer to discover that if all the "bads" grow exponentially and all the "goods" arithmetically or not at all, catastrophe will inevitably result.

The reply to this criticism is predictable. The reports maintain that: (1) the assumptions of a fivefold increase in resources and a fourfold reduction in pollution generation are liberal; (2) the overshoot and collapse mode always recurs after an interval of time; (3) the economic process to be effective must operate in coordinated fashion on all five variables—a tall order for a process that heretofore has not been conspicuously holistic; (4) technological solutions frequently beget serious new problems; and (5) time delays make the discovery of side effects and the implementation of technical solutions problematic.

The Limits to Growth maintains that some problems exist for which there are no technical solutions,[18] while Forrester insists that as limits are approached, there will be less maneuvering room for technological solutions. In such situations technological solutions may more and more be only the substitution of one crisis for another. *The Limits to Growth* concludes:

We have felt it necessary to dwell so long on an analysis of technology here because we have found that technological optimism is the most common and the most dangerous reaction to our findings from the world model. Technology can relieve the symptoms of a problem without affecting the underlying causes. Faith in technology as the ultimate solution to all problems can thus divert our attention from the most fundamental problem—the problem of growth in a finite system—and prevent us from taking effective action to solve it.[19]

Does the technological process push limits back exponentially? We can only point to the ambiguity of the evidence, note the disagreement among those who are in the best position to make assessments, and finally admit that we do not know. Nevertheless, we must insist that the question is of immense significance, not to be decided simply on the basis of how one feels about technology.

Perhaps we need also to recover the neglected virtue of prudence. To proceed on the basis of growth while hoping for technological solutions may be prudent. The social adjustments in shifting to an equilibrium economy may be so problematic that growth is perhaps the better option. But what are the consequences if the present course is maintained and technological solutions are not sufficient? The M.I.T. reports insist that there will be immense human suffering. This should at least be a sobering prospect not taken too lightly. The main risk in the growth option is severe economic and population crises, after which it may not be possible to reestablish anything but a marginal existence for a remnant. Balanced against this risk is the possibility of considerable gains for the poor and marginal gains of questionable value for the already affluent. We should stress the word "possibility," for the growth option carries with it the continued dominance of economic and technological values into the foreseeable future, a dominance that seems to require the disproportionate distribution of income and wealth. Thus the gains for the poor may not be so great.

Alternatively, the risk of the equilibrium option is potential social strife and nonrealization of potential gains from growth in the short run. However, it is important to see that the nonrealization of growth dividends would only be a short-run phenomenon if the futurists are wrong. The growth process could probably be activated once again if it is determined that the earth could sustain higher levels of economic activity than the futurists project. In comparison, restarting the growth machine would probably be much more difficult after overshoot and collapse.

Given our present information, the prudent course seems to be in the direction of an equilibrium economy. Increasingly, observers of long-range prospects agree that at some point in the future, equilibrium is inevitable. For many of these observers, however, the more significant questions are, How near are the limits? and, What level of economic activity could be sustained over a long period? The answer to the first is the primary guide to what must be done now. If we are far short of the limits, there is little need for immediate corrective action. If we are close to the limits, then immediate steps seem warranted. Unfortunately, there are considerable differences of opinion on this question. As for the amount of production and consumption that is sustainable, on the answer to this rests the resolution of several social and ethical questions.

So what do we do? For several reasons, restricting the growth process seems to be the best option. First, the consequences of being wrong are far greater when the laissez-faire approach is taken. Second, the equilibrium economy may be more desirable than it looks at first glance. It may present a real option to the industrialized countries, whether or not it is actually becoming necessary. Finally, we are more likely to find answers to pressing questions by taking steps toward equilibrium. Such steps would at minimum include the cessation of population growth, the restriction of environmentally destructive technologies, the reduction of the current rapid growth in the use of power, a shift in consumption patterns, the focus of new technologies on pollution control, movement toward recycling and durability, and finally redistribution.

Ethical Implications

Reviewers of the M.I.T. reports often point out that they make little effort to deal with the profound social, political, and ethical implications of their projections. Some go on to raise the ideological issues. They accuse the team of propagating a conservative, escapist, and "kick-the-ladder-down-behind-you" ideology.

These charges miss the real openness of team members to all of the issues involved. Indeed, the M.I.T. study is radical in its implications. Much the same can be said for the work of Mesarovic and Pestel and other futurists. They call into question the entire thrust for growth and raise to greater intensity almost every ethical issue thus far discussed.

Perhaps the best example is the issue of redistribution. If the futurists are correct in saying that the technological "fix" will be unable to stave off limits, the convenient alternative of an ever-larger pie will no longer mute criticism of the existing distribution. The pie will be roughly constant, and the issue of redistribution will not so easily be covered over by rising incomes. This applies equally for distribution within a given country and distribution throughout the world. Closely linked is the problem of social strife and international warfare over scarce resources.

In addition to intensifying familiar ethical issues, the futurists introduce several new ones. Consider, for example, the problem of the future itself and the implied question, Why should we be concerned about our grandchildren? The problem arises because of the present tendency in most countries to focus on the present or very near future and to neglect the longer-range outlook. This focus is too narrow, as the logic of exponential growth with its rapid doubling times should warn us. Mesarovic and Pestel, in particular, stress the tragic loss of life and tremendous added expense that will result from unnecessary delays.[20] Contrary to past assumptions, they warn us, time is not on our side.

The problem runs even deeper. Why should we be worried about the future at all? It is often said: "Each generation has to take care of itself"; "I won't be around, so why should I worry?"; or even, "Consider the lilies of the field; . . . they neither toil nor spin." However appealing such statements are to the sense of fatalism we all feel, they fly in the face of an equally appealing sense of concern for the future and the needs of posterity. This concern is embodied in Edmund Burke's ongoing view of society in which ancestors and posterity are seen as sharing in the decisions of the present. The present takes in trust a gift from the past with the responsibility of passing it on in no worse condition than that in which it was received. This view in essence is the Christian ethical notion of stewardship.

A concern for posterity is also one aspect of Christian love, of Christian responsibility to God and neighbor. Our response to the love of God includes responsibility for the material and cultural condition of posterity. Our grandchildren and our neighbor's grandchildren, even though remote in time and space, are still our neighbors. Jesus' saying that the lilies neither toil nor spin is not a counsel to neglect, but a call to faith. It tells us not to be *anxious* about the future. Nowhere does God say, Sit back, I'll take care of the mess you have made. Rather it is abundantly clear that God has given us freedom and calls us to respond in faith to his love. God will not bail us out, even though his love is always with us.

Clearly, the weight of Christian ethical judgment lies on the side of a concern and responsibility for posterity. The burden of responsibility is placed all the more on the present because posterity has no power in present decisions. Our grandchildren are subject to our decisions without representation.

Yet we must admit realistically that the needs of the present are almost always more compelling. Given food shortages, material destitution, or unemployment in the present, the initial ethical response is to do everything possible to help. Indeed, human suffering is usually so compelling that the policymaker has little recourse but to devote resources to the problem. But if the M.I.T. team is correct, such action may tragically set the stage for greater human suffering, since ultimately limits will be reached with a larger population and perhaps fewer resources.

A call to responsibility for the future contains no suggestion that the present should be disregarded. On the contrary, the initial ethical response—to relieve suffering—in most cases will be the correct one. The future is too full of contingencies to let it rule in a situation of widespread misery. But the point is that, even in cases that are not extreme, we have insufficiently taken into account the needs of the future. Suffering caused by lack of food and squalid conditions is not characteristic of all the world's people. In fact, the majority of Americans do not suffer material deprivation. Yet they consume and produce with little thought of future generations.

Furthermore, we can say that insensitivity to the needs of the future impoverishes the present. Love is more fully actualized in the present when we act with love toward the future. Sensitivity and care in one area carries over into others. This is the essential dynamic of God's love.

It is also the message of Christian eschatology, the focus of which is the present as well as the future. The second coming of Christ is an event in the life of each person. "The time is fulfilled, and the kingdom of God is at hand; repent and believe in the gospel." This is the great summation of Jesus' message (Mark 1:15). While future-oriented, his message also has its focus on the present. That is, the new person is actualized in love by the inbreaking and soon-to-be-realized kingdom of God.

The hope and the promise of a better future actualizes the present. It provides the motivation to realize ever-higher levels of justice and love. And this is true whether it be Thomas More's utopia, Marx's classless society, Jesus' kingdom of God, or simply the statement, "I care about how my children will live." We are spiritually dead without the hope and promise of a better future.

The United States is an example of a country that has grown presumptuous in its prosperity. It neglects suffering in both the present and the future. The little hardship that might be incurred, for example, by the increased costs of pollution control or more foreign assistance, could be borne with relative ease. Yet, despite this insight, there is strong resistance. We simply do not consider the future with anywhere near the same concentration we give to the present. Even in the present we ignore the poor among us and throughout the world. Easy assumptions about progressive growth have let us off the hook and blinded us to both present and future crises.

To change this pattern of neglect we must either revitalize our utopian and eschatological symbols or create new ones. Such symbols must combine the spiritual with the material, for both are brought into question by the futurists. Thus, for example, the kingdom of God as an eschatological symbol requires at least a tentative material embodiment to accompany its spiritual revitalization.

Finally, this reconsideration of the future includes a concrete ethical dilemma. Jay Forrester raised it in an address to the Division of Overseas Ministries of the National Council of Churches: Imagine two countries, country L and country S. On the one hand, assume that country L has a long-range outlook, not allowing population and industry to grow at a faster rate than can be maintained within the natural capacity of ecosystems and willing to accept short-term penalties to maintain an equilibrium of ecosystems. On the other hand, assume that country S lives for the present only and allows population and industry to grow without restriction. What will be the responsibility of country L to country S at the point where S requests assistance because it has exhausted its environment and cannot maintain its population? Is country L to pay twice for the profligacy of country S, once by forgoing present consumption and again by assisting S? Indeed, if country S can count on L for aid, why shouldn't it pursue a policy oriented to maximize present gain?

The irony of Forrester's example is that it is the reversal of what has traditionally counted as wise economic policy. Up to now forgoing consumption in order to accumulate capital was the best policy for the future. Forrester retains the aspect of forgoing consumption in the present. But this forgoing of consumption is not for the purpose of constructing additional industrial capacity; it is for the maintenance of ecosystems. It is the forgoing of both consumption and investment. In addition, continuing to use Forrester's example, traditional wisdom has maintained that country L would be coming to S for assistance in the future, that is, aid to underdeveloped countries.

This dilemma once again underscores the degree to which crises now on the horizon challenge accepted wisdom and call for global cooperation. For one scientist, one nation, or one region to go it alone will no longer suffice in the face of such gigantic problems. The task of anyone concerned with both present and future is to try to avoid tragic choices. We must, through increased attention to these future problems, avoid a situation where country L refuses food or other aid to country S, thinking that it is thereby preventing greater calamities in the future.

This sort of ethical dilemma reinforces the call for a changed attitude toward economic growth, toward the future, and toward international consequences of social policies. The futurists' projections may not be the path of the future. But the consequences of proceeding on laissez-faire assumptions are far worse.

Yet such appeals are essentially negative. Perhaps the equilibrium economy is more than a tool to avoid catastrophe. Perhaps it is positive possibility, a constructive alternative way to realize a better future.

Chapter 8

THE SUSTAINABLE
SOCIETY

Three alternatives face us, claim the authors of *The Limits to Growth*: (1) unrestricted growth; (2) a self-imposed limitation of growth; (3) a nature-imposed limitation of growth.[1] Of these, only the second and third are actually possible. If the third is selected, the present course of unrestricted growth will lead to uncontrollable population growth on the one hand and capital decrease on the other. If the second is selected, we are faced with the enormous task of radically reordering our economic system, our political structures, and the reigning ideology of the past two hundred years.

What such a radical reordering might entail, assuming the second option is selected, is beginning to emerge in general outline.[2] Kenneth Boulding compares the re-ordered society to a spaceship. A 1974 conference of the World Council of Churches called for a "sustainable society." Others envision an "equilibrium" or "no-growth" economy.

Whatever we call the reordering, it will necessarily have economic, political, and ethical components. Perhaps the term "sustainable society" best conveys the overall reordering, while "equilibrium economy" is best used to refer only to the economic component. Thus we have the whole, the sustainable society, requiring an equilibrium economy; a globally oriented, yet decentralized, political system; and a new world view.

The Equilibrium Economy

Assuming that the futurists are correct, there are two possible ways to avert limits and the suffering that probably would accompany them. The option we now rely on works primarily through the technological process to reduce or eliminate constraints on growth. Alternatively, we have the option of restricting or reducing the factors that produce expansion.

The hypothetical equilibrium economy follows the second path without rejecting the first. In the words of the M.I.T. study, it would be an economy in which "population and capital are essentially stable, with the forces tending to increase or decrease them in carefully controlled balance." [3] More specifically, it would be an economy in which population and annual product would be (1) sustainable indefinitely without sudden and uncontrollable collapse and (2) capable of meeting the basic material needs of *all* people. Such an economy would necessarily be in equilibrium with basic ecological support systems and would minimize, not maximize, the consumption of nonrenewable resources. It would not, however, be an economy in which growth is entirely eliminated. Rather, it would be an economy of differentiated growth, one that concentrates on nonpolluting and nondepleting forms of economic activity and aims at the two goals of environmental soundness and contribution to human welfare.

What did it take to avoid limits and to produce equilibrium in the M.I.T. model? It is noteworthy that equilibrium resulted only with significant reductions in pollution generation and natural resource usage. The M.I.T. team also arrived at a minimum set of general requirements for global equilibrium:

> 1. *The capital plant and the population are constant in size.* The birth rate equals the death rate and the capital investment rate equals the depreciation rate.
>
> 2. *All input and output—births, deaths, investment, and depreciation—are kept to a minimum.*
>
> 3. *The levels of capital and population and the ratio of the two are set in accordance with the values of society.* They may be deliberately revised and slowly adjusted as the advance of technology creates new options.[4]

This equilibrium, the team maintains, could and should be a "dynamic equilibrium." Adjustments in population size and capital stock within the limits of long-range equilibrium could easily be made to reflect changed preferences. Increases in both would be possible through technological innovations. The equilibrium economy need not be stagnant or stifling.

Mesarovic and Pestel do not speculate directly about the equilibrium economy. They call for differentiated growth, but point out that a "master plan" has yet to evolve. The heart of their work is the devising of strategies to solve the many problems associated with economic and population growth. For the three problems of economic development, resource shortage, and food production, they ran several resolving strategies through their computer. The results are significant. Only strategies that involved immediate action, worldwide cooperation, a long-range perspective, and balanced economic development among the world's regions were successful in avoiding crisis. Consider, for example, their summary of the food problem:

> The only feasible solution to the world food situation requires:
>
> 1. A global approach to the problem.
> 2. Investment aid rather than commodity aid, except for food.
> 3. A balanced economic development for all regions.
> 4. An effective population policy.
> 5. Worldwide diversification of industry, leading to a truly global economic system.
>
> Only a proper combination of these measures can lead to a solution. Omissions of any one measure will surely lead to disaster. But the strains on the global food production capacity would be lessened if the eating habits in the affluent part of the world would change, becoming less wasteful.[5]

It is necessary to consider the work of economist Herman E. Daly for greater detail on the equilibrium economy itself. Daly, whose work antedates the M.I.T. reports, has speculated in some depth about the equilibrium economy, which he calls the "stationary-state economy." [6] The basic requirements of the stationary-state economy would be a constant stock of physical wealth (capital) and a constant number of people (population). Obviously capital and population do not remain constant by themselves. People die, capital equipment wears out. The stocks of capital and numbers of people must be maintained by new production and births. In the stationary-state economy the rates of new production and births would exactly equal the rates of consumption and death. This contrasts with present growth patterns, where inflow exceeds outflow, resulting in economic and population growth.

Nevertheless, equality may be achieved with a high or low turnover rate. For example, we can maintain a constant population with birth and death rates that are either both high or both low. A description of the stationary-state economy is not complete until the turnover rate is specified. In the stationary-state economy this rate should be as low as possible, argues Daly. Drawing on the image of water flowing through a tank, Daly observes that the faster the water flows, the less time an average drop spends in the tank. Likewise in terms of population, a low rate of flow or turnover means low birth rates, low death rates, longer life expectancy, and a population with a higher average age. Similarly for stocks of capital, a low rate of flow means lower production, lower consumption, higher durability, older equipment on the average, and increased recycling of materials.

These specifications may mean more leisure time because of lower production rates. Daly, for one, seems to think so. But others, notably British economist E. F. Schumacher, feel there should be a partial return to small-scale, labor-intensive production. People, not machines, would increasingly do the labor; and laboring would take place in small enough units to ensure permanence, a humanized technology, and easy accessibility.[7]

Echoing Schumacher, a few representatives from developing nations now claim that the mass importation into their countries of Western technology and growth patterns is catastrophic. Indian economist Samuel L. Parmar argues that the main cause of both Third World subservience and the growing strain on nonrenewable resources is the acceptance of consumerism, giantism, rapid industrialization, and advanced technology.[8] Parmar calls for self-reliance by Third World nations. For most developing countries this would mean the continuation and promotion of labor-intensive production, simple manufacturing processes, and less dependence on Western technology. Indeed, this pattern might well characterize the equilibrium economy itself.

Actually the situation might not be an "either" of leisure with high technology balanced against an "or" of physical work and labor-intensive production. The technological process will yield improvements that increase durability, use fewer resources, and decrease pollution. These improvements would permit gradually increasing stocks of capital and perhaps even numbers of people. Daly's minimization policy is not entirely accurate. Yes, the goals of the equilibrium economy will be durability, recycling, and longevity with a minimum of production and consumption. But this minimum is best guided by the criteria of environmental soundness and human welfare. Production, consumption, and employment of laborsaving technology can be increased as long as these criteria are satisfied. Needless to say, the provision of most "services" could be expanded indefinitely. Even so, most futurists feel that production and consumption consistent with environmental soundness will be at substantially lower levels than those current in most industrial countries.

Reducing levels of production and consumption suggests several problems. Actually what we can see is only the tip of the iceberg. We should not be deceived by simple outlines. Little conceptual work has been done, and only a few of the more outstanding problems have even been identified. The futurists must be considered visionaries at this point. Perhaps a brief summary of just a few problems will give us an idea of what may be in store.

To start with, several items will present themselves for decision. What is an equilibrium size of capital and people? What is a desirable turnover rate? Should we be many people consuming little or a few consuming much? At what point do we reach diminishing returns with recycling and durability? Indeed, what shifts will be required in the changeover to durability, recycling, and labor-intensive, small-scale production? To answer bluntly, we don't know.

Undoubtedly there will be considerable unemployment and initial dislocation. An endless number of interrelated variables must be kept straight. Ways to maintain education, medicine, and certain leisure industries must be found. Incentives will require restructuring. It will be necessary to reorient and mute our intense competitive drives. The problems of a generally older population, including a possible loss of youthful spirit, will quickly become apparent. We will need to revamp our entire transportation system, doing away with the automobile as our primary means of transportation and substituting modes that consume less energy. This in turn will have profound implications for our suburban patterns of living. And if these problems are not enough, we need only note the fantastic costs in money and resources. Societies simply do not change their economic patterns without costs. There is no such thing as a free lunch.

Political Portents

A shift of such magnitude will inevitably produce political conflict. How intense this conflict will be depends in large measure on how rapidly a new consciousness develops. The manned space flight program was relatively easy to execute, once the will for it became clear. In the case of the sustainable society no comparable consensus exists at present. Thus the political struggle is likely to be intense. Vested interests, not to mention established attitudes, will be challenged and threatened.

A major source of conflict will be the distribution of income and wealth, unless the sustainable society is instituted in a repressive manner. The size of the pie will be constant, not growing. The present covering-over effect of growth will vanish and the issue will be out in the open. Even more, the implementation of such measures as pollution control, taxes, the inclusion of social costs, and the elimination of industries that are intensively polluting and depleting will have a regressive effect on income unless countermeasures are taken.

Hence, on the one hand, the poor majority will be less likely to accept existing differentials and will resist any efforts to push the costs of establishing equilibrium onto them. On the other hand, the wealthy few will seek to preserve existing differentials and to push the costs onto the poor. Such a drawing of lines has rather obvious implications for political conflict. This goes equally well for nations as for individuals.

Competition for scarce resources will be intensified both nationally and internationally. Wars can be expected, for example, when one nation limits exports of a scarce commodity in order to promote its own domestic equilibrium or to conserve for the welfare of future generations. Already the threat of war over scarce oil reserves is upon us. Veiled threats of military intervention, to be carried out in case of certain provocations, may well be a foretaste of things to come. Tragically, wars will have a ruinous effect on equilibrium, thus adding to the difficulties.

This leads inevitably to a consideration of worldwide political organizations. The sustainable society will require a more internationally oriented political system. The present system of autonomous national units would seem to be ill-suited to the need. Among other things, it would be unable to control the many variables involved in the sustainable society and unable to prevent the competition for scarce resources from leading to ruinous wars.

One aspect of this political problem is the question of the relative merits of centralization and decentralization. E. F. Schumacher proclaims that "small is beautiful." And "A Blueprint for Survival" argues for decentralization, self-sufficiency, and small economic units. On the obvious possibilities of decentralization, it adds:

> It would . . . be sensible to promote the social conditions in which public opinion and full public participation in decision-making become as far as possible the means whereby communities are ordered. The larger a community the less likely this can be: in a heterogeneous, centralized society such as ours, the restraints of the stable society if they were to be effective would appear as so much outside

coercion; but in communities small enough for the general will to be worked out and expressed by individuals confident of themselves and their fellows as individuals, "us and them" situations are less likely to occur—people having learned the limits of a stable society would be free to order their own lives within them as they wished, and would therefore accept the restraints of the stable society as necessary and desirable and not as some arbitrary restriction imposed by a remote and unsympathetic government.[9]

In the long run a greater degree of decentralization appears to be the only alternative. From a political perspective, however, decentralization has several drawbacks. It is potentially anarchic. It is vulnerable to exploitation by individual units. It cannot ensure that all small units will pursue an equilibrium policy. It encourages an uneven distribution of the world's resources. In fact, a decentralized, autonomous system would almost inevitably produce a skewed distribution of wealth, if for no other reason than that natural wealth itself is widely and unevenly distributed. Nor could all small units be self-sufficient, because there are critical shortages in given areas. Some sort of international trade would thus be required, and this in turn would necessitate some form of international organization.

In sum, the decentralization envisioned by Schumacher and by "A Blueprint for Survival" is shortsighted. It overlooks certain fundamental aspects of human nature, lends itself to the imperialism of the strong, and is vulnerable to a "feudal solution" in which the rich exploit the poor.

While this is true, centralization seems to offer little by way of an alternative. On the positive side, a centralized organization could provide the controls necessary to prevent ruinous wars and to regulate the equilibrium structure. It might also help to prevent a feudal solution, provided there is some degree of democratic decision-making. Nor would centralization necessarily presuppose a complete change of attitudes.

While centralization provides a better means of control, it opens up awesome possibilities for tyranny. The prospect of uniting world political and economic power under one roof is frightening. Nor is there any guarantee whatever that such a system would lead to redistribution. Maldistribution is just as likely in a centralized structure as in a decentralized one.

But the most intractable problem of all would be the control of nuclear weapons. Here we are on the horns of what is perhaps an unsolvable dilemma. Nuclear weapons would be almost impossible to control in a decentralized system. This also means that the equilibrium economy would be almost impossible to control, since any political unit with nuclear autonomy would be free to go its own way. To control equilibrium the power over nuclear weapons would probably have to be centralized in some fashion. To economic and political power would be added nuclear power. The sum of the three comes very close to equaling absolute power and, as the old adage goes, absolute power corrupts absolutely.

Only the most presumptuous would attempt to offer comprehensive solutions to these dilemmas. It is conceivable, however, that after a period of centrally enforced restrictions, an evolving world view congenial to the sustainable society would permit loosening and decentralization. It is also conceivable that some sort of federation with checks and balances might develop—that is, a structural solution which could either be centralized or decentralized, but in which structures and attitudes are developed to deal effectively with the intrinsic limitations of the system selected.

In sum, neither is satisfactory in itself. The problem is not so much a choice between centralization and decentralization as it is the definition and development of various types of centralization and decentralization. Either, like growth, can be differentiated. Either would probably work, provided there is a will for the sustainable society and cooperation. Neither will work if this will is absent.

In the end some sort of mix will probably emerge. A globally oriented authority will be necessary to manage a worldwide sustainable society, to ensure a just distribution, and to prevent ruinous wars. But over the long haul this centralization must be balanced by some sort of decentralization of power and the development of small, integrated communities where personal interaction can develop. The specter of a worldwide and highly rationalized bureaucracy too easily suggests the horrors of Orwell's *1984*. In any case we will be forced to walk the tightrope between anarchy and repression, freedom and coercion.

Needed: A New World View

Garrett Hardin, in his well-known essay "The Tragedy of the Commons," identifies a class of problems that have no technical solution. His proposal for dealing with these problems is political: "mutual coercion mutually agreed upon." Political scientist Beryl Crowe, reflecting on Hardin's solution, argues there are problems with no political solution. Indeed, he claims Hardin's "mutual coercion mutually agreed upon" is politically impossible.[10] If Hardin and Crowe together are correct, the "commons problem" cannot be solved by technical and political means alone.

In arguing that undifferentiated growth has limits, the futurists are in effect saying that a "commons problem" is before us. Their solution, of course, is the sustainable society. But if the solution is not a technical or a political possibility, where are we to find the resources for implementation? Is there no recourse but to proceed along a path leading to human suffering as nature imposes the limits we are unable to avoid?

This sort of speculation has a macabre quality to it. But we are not without resources. There is no *a priori* reason why we must be resigned to the determinism of nature-imposed limits. What Hardin and Crowe are really saying is this: assuming undifferentiated growth to be a "commons problem," neither technical nor political solutions *alone* will suffice. This is not to say technology and politics will play no role. They are key factors in any viable solution. Rather, it is to say that there must be a critical third component, a new world view involving a radical change of attitudes and values, before the sustainable society will become a reality.

This is a tall order. John Maynard Keynes, reflecting on his projection of future unlimited abundance leading to ever-increasing leisure, stated, "I think with dread of the readjustment of habits and instincts of the ordinary man, bred into him for countless generations, which he may be asked to discard within a few decades." [11] Keynes's dread applies even more to the sustainable society. While critically important, the achievement of a new world view is the most difficult task of all.

The outlines and directions of a new world view or ethic are beginning to emerge. It is and must be a world view that reverses the present quasi-religious commitment to growth. It has two tasks: the criticism of the reigning ethic and the construction of an alternative. In these tasks Christians may find real opportunities to contribute.

1. One starting point is an appreciation of nature. Several recent philosophical and theological studies have started at precisely this point. Though they differ markedly in approach and content, they have in common both a deep appreciation of nature and a strong criticism of the now popular instrumental view of nature. Any theological or philosophical reconstruction must at least rectify the currently destructive imbalance that has resulted in Western culture from a too-narrow emphasis on man as the measure of all things.

Theologically, Christians have work to do if they are to play a significant role in this renewed appreciation of nature. Christians have neglected nature by a too-exclusive emphasis on God and man. Nature simply hasn't received equal time in the tradition; and even when it has, the attention received has mostly cast nature as an instrument of inferior status.

Not only has nature been neglected, but Christian views have played a significant, though ambiguous, part in the use and continuing importance of science, technology, and economic expansion. This is not so much a judgment on Christian thought as it is a frank awareness of its ideological role. Christians have given a boost to the material and ideological forces underlying economic growth through their general emphases, their themes of subduing and having dominion in Genesis, their desacralization of nature, and their natural theology. Moreover, this ideological role continues today, even though Christianity has only a marginal social influence and dominant attitudes toward nature have little explicit Christian content. If nothing else, Christians have in recent times acquiesced in the exploitation of nature.

One way for Christians to begin is by reassessing the dominion and stewardship themes in Genesis. To have dominion and subdue the earth meant one thing to the ancient Hebrews, who for all their faults could not be accused of endangering the global environment. In our time, when nature gods are no longer the threat they were to the Hebrews, the themes have become vehicles of pride and idolatry. It is time to relax our subduing. "Dominion" does not mean destruction. It implies loving stewardship, a meaning that a careful reading of the dominion texts in Genesis indicates was also intended by the Hebrews. "Stewardship" is care for the earth and compassion for persons. And while the steward too easily becomes the slave overseer, this should not be an excuse for jettisoning this strong Biblical notion. Stewardship, for all its dangers, conveys man's actual relationship to nature. We are part of nature, yet stand outside of it, control it, and have the ability to interfere in it. Interfering in nature cannot be abolished. A return to nature in denial of transcendence will not solve our problems. The call of Genesis and the tradition is rather to care, to have compassion, and to exercise a just stewardship.

2. An implicit religion of growth with its accompanying exploitation of nature pervades our society. This fact should not be obscured by academic arguments, such as the question whether this religion of growth is a

consequence or a betrayal of Christianity. The questioning of this implicit religion raises the specter of an ideological crisis. The way we have put our ideas together for several centuries is now cast into radical doubt. The crisis is profoundly religious, for there is an absence of religious sensitivity in our preoccupation with affluence. The perception of crisis reaches to our deepest self-identities.

This perception of crisis is heightened by the weakness in practice of alternative philosophies and religious understandings. Christians as well as humanists have bought into the religion of growth at a fearful cost—the loss of their own spiritual and prophetic traditions. Perhaps it is now time to view this implicit religion of growth as idolatrous, as another example in the long line of human pride. We have given free reign to avarice and exploitation and have divorced our deepest spiritual values from our activity in the world. Nor is it too much to view the environmental crisis and projections of future human suffering as warnings of God's impending judgment on our pride and idolatry.

Where do we turn? For Christians the answer is clear. The call of God is to repentance and reconciliation in Jesus Christ, a call which in the present circumstances is hard to hear and harder still to answer. Concretely it is a call to basics: to faith; to human appeals for food, clothing, shelter, and health; to liberating structures that provide opportunities for human cooperation and creativity; to the throwing off of enslaving forces of affluence. The cross of the present crisis is not the final word. Out of death comes new life. Jesus Christ has overthrown the enslaving powers. We are free to change our ways without fear of judgment, for God is with us.

3. Our view of nature and our religious understandings are only two of many subjects for reassessment. Attitudes toward work, consumption, and abundance must all be reconsidered. The myths surrounding science and technology must be punctured and new, more satisfying myths created. To counter the influence of the technostructure, nontechnical and noneconomic values must be raised up.

Here also we must reconsider mass production and the substitution of machine power for human labor. With E. F. Schumacher, perhaps we should have as one goal an "intermediate technology," which provides first-class tools to a system of production intensive in labor. Schumacher calls it "technology with a human face."

> The system of production by the masses mobilizes the priceless resources which are possessed by all human beings, their clever brains and skillful hands, and supports them with first-class tools. The technology of mass production is inherently violent, ecologically damaging, self-defeating in terms of non-renewable resources, and stultifying for the human person. The technology of production by the masses, making use of modern knowledge and experience, is conducive to decentralization, compatible with the laws of ecology, gentle in its use of scarce resources, and designed to serve the human person instead of making him the servant of machines.[12]

That Schumacher's vision would be adaptable to all regions is not clear. Herman E. Daly thinks a serious problem in the industrialized nations will be how to share the work, or, on the other side of the coin, how to use the new leisure created by a slackening demand for labor. He assumes the continuation of advanced technology, although one scrubbed of its environmentally unsound elements. The difference between Schumacher and Daly confuses the picture. If human labor is emphasized, as in Schumacher, then many of the attitudes associated with the so-called Protestant work ethic will apply. Alternatively, if advanced technology dominates, then we will need to develop a leisure ethic and a work-sharing ethic. This picture is further confused by the obvious need for considerable labor to bring the sustainable society into being. Yet, while we retain many of our present hardworking attitudes, we will need to redirect them; to eliminate the obsessive aspects of some work habits, the felt need to work in order to consume, and the alienating character of much labor. To give order to this bewildering array of considerations is not possible at present. But the confusion does point to the concern of many that we will end up with a sense of meaninglessness where no one feels called to work for the common good.

However unclear the work picture is, new consuming styles will be essential. The present waste of energy, food, and natural resources in the United States must end if there be any hope for the sustainable society. Schumacher says "small is beautiful," which points to the minimization policy we need. Not, "How much can we get?" but, "How little do we really need?" will be the consuming question. All of which implies a revolutionary new pattern of life with staggering implications in the United States.

4. Alternative solutions to the problems for which growth has historically provided the answers must be developed in this new world view. This means a face-to-face confrontation with the international and national realities of distribution, freedom and coercion, social strife, employment, and the potential consequences of a

declining standard of living. This also means the development of an alternative world view to deal with these problems. Finally, this means a criticism of present cost accounting and changed perceptions of social costs.

But above all, ethical resources must be found for dealing with the increased domestic and international conflict which the equilibrium economy makes a very real possibility. Natural resource shortages and overcrowding alone will create numerous occasions for conflict. Equally significant, the continuation of present expenditures to support military establishments (over $200 billion annually throughout the world) and the continuation of present levels of international and domestic conflict would destroy the possibility of the sustainable society.

No more urgent task confronts us than that of shifting from conflict to cooperation. Human beings have always yearned for the day when swords would be beaten into plowshares, cheeks would instinctively be turned, and all persons would be good Samaritans. Today these images of perfect harmony need to be more than hopes. And while perfect peace is nowhere on the horizon, much ground can be covered before our ethical resources are exhausted.

Unfortunately, cooperation frequently means the sacrifice of immediate, personal gains for a hypothetically better future for all. Thus cooperation for Americans probably means reduced material consumption now so that poorer nations may grow, to the long-range betterment of all. This call to reduce consumption for the sake of cooperation is unprecedented. It taxes our ethical resources to the utmost.

In short, the sustainable society increases the likelihood of conflict at a time when present ethical and political resources are wrongly ordered to produce the peace which the society necessarily presupposes. Only a new world view involving both in thought and deed the widespread renunciation of force *and* injustice will be sufficient for this new situation.

5. Within the new world view there must occur a reversal of the current emphasis on quantity over quality, means over ends, structures over values, and the individual over the commons—all characteristic of the growth-advocacy position. Equally important, the new view will necessarily direct our attention to longer-range problems. What is needed is not a total shift from the present to the long-range, but a greater degree of balance. The new world view must consider the entire time span. We must, for example, weigh immediate benefits more carefully against long-range impacts and vice versa.

A concern for future generations is raised to much greater importance by the projections of the futurists. At present a vague and largely unarticulated concern exists. The new world view must go far beyond just a vague concern. It must point to the personhood of our grandchildren, to the need for a heightened stewardship in an enlarged definition of the situation, and to the insensitivity produced now by the neglect of the future.

Here the proponents of the new may find help in the current trend toward theologies of the future. We do not mean those theologies which seek a simple solution to the world's problems, undercutting the will to create more just institutions. Rather, we are referring to those which face the full range of possible responses to God's love and attempt to point concretely to where God may be at

work. Too often much of God's work is overlooked
because we fail to flesh out our theologies with real
possibilities.

From a theological standpoint we affirm that God will
be at work in the future through love to bring into being
more just social institutions and new relationships of
persons to nature. But God's work of justice and love is
always concretely embodied—as, for example, in the
incarnation. Indeed, we are called to respond in acts of
love, not in abstract affirmations.

Thus it is not sufficient merely to affirm that God will
be at work in the future. It is also necessary to make
concrete, though *tentative,* judgments about his presence.
It is necessary to outline tentative utopias that envision
new societies and new relationships to nature as the
material embodiments of abstract eschatology. For
the new world view this means serious consideration of
the sustainable society as one possible embodiment of
God's love.

Equally important is the development and communication of a persuasive basis for hope. The past two
centuries have seen a close link between hope, optimism,
and a sense of vitality on the one hand, and material
increase on the other. Because of this link, the specter of
the end of the lode may easily lead to pessimism,
nihilism, and "loss of nerve." It is of little use to say that
material increase has been a false, even idolatrous, goal.
The fact is, this link has been strong, and the breaking of
it is fraught with complications.

The new world view will therefore have to develop a
new basis for hope, optimism, and vitality. And to use
the word "new" is not to suggest that an entirely original
ethic must be carved out of virgin timber. Ample

resources are available within the Christian tradition to provide a sound basis. The word "new" would indicate the shifting away from the present world view, which is dominated by economic and technical considerations.

6. Finally, even if the futurists are wrong, there are compelling reasons to shift from a "growth" to a "sustainable" world view. Many elements of the sustainable society are desirable in their own right. They are needed correctives for present social injustice and callousness, and for the tendency to give primary attention to economic and technologically based values. The world view outlined here is therefore not merely an antidote for the problems of limits; just as important, it is a suggestive new ethical direction. The proponents of the sustainable society would do well to insist, as their first priority, that the new society offer at least as many possibilities as problems.

Chapter 9

PROBLEMS AND POSSIBILITIES

Adequate trails cannot be mapped until both present position and destination have been fixed. If the futurists are correct, we know roughly where we are and vaguely where we should be heading. Unfortunately our map is lacking in detail, our means of transportation have not been requisitioned, and there is grave doubt whether the terrain can be negotiated. But now that we have a vague idea of that destination, let us briefly consider the route and the possibilities of arriving before the monsoon.

What route should the industrial nations take in the face of the many ethical, political, and economic difficulties? Two basic alternatives seem available. (1) Let present trends continue. Do little, hoping there is yet plenty of time or that the technological process will save the day; (2) Take as many steps as "possible" toward the sustainable society, never letting the "possible" limit imagination, or social pessimism undercut the imperative for action.

Immediate Steps

Given the foregoing analysis, the second seems the only sensible alternative. Concretely, this means in the short run taking a variety of steps whose purpose is twofold—to move us toward the new society and to put us in a better position to assess what will eventually be required. Several steps come immediately to mind:

1. Basic research into the effects of pollution, the continuing availability of resources, and the possibilities of resource substitution.
2. Programs to restrict population increase, with particular emphasis in developed countries on voluntary contraception.
3. Programs to encourage new technologies designed to extend resources and suppress pollution, with special emphasis on durability, recycling, and differentiated growth.
4. The elimination of heavily polluting and depleting productive processes.
5. A coordinated resource policy.
6. Movement toward a more equitable distribution of income, wealth, and social costs; followed by the elimination of wasteful food, resource, and energy consumption.
7. Programs to compensate for dislocations and unemployment.
8. Cultivation of changing attitudes through new visions that concentrate on (*a*) the fragility of the planet, and (*b*) the positive aspects of the sustainable society.

To implement even these minimal steps we must begin

with voluntary measures and institute increasingly coercive measures only as the situation warrants. We should also seek international coordination of efforts, remembering from earlier discussions the interrelatedness of the problems, and the insight that what may be a corrective in one region might create problems in another.

Will these eight steps, or others that could be added, be sufficient? No one can tell, but they are a starting point at which to begin the task of determining what will eventually be necessary. Since time is a critical factor, there should be no delay in starting.

Steps for the longer range depend on the length of time before limits are reached, the final level of equilibrium, and what is done now. Unfortunately, these steps are impossible to delineate, since only minimal plans are now being made, and very little is known about time limits and equilibrium levels.

Is the Transition Possible?

What about the transition to the sustainable society? Is it a real possibility? Socialist Michael Harrington and economist Robert L. Heilbroner have grave doubts.

Michael Harrington draws on the Marxist tradition. Marxism has consistently denied that the "estrangement" of the present economic system can be overcome without the fullest development of productive forces—that is, without abundance. Marx himself in *The German Ideology* states:

> This "estrangement" . . . can, of course, only be abolished given two *practical* premises. For it to become an "intolerable" power, i.e., a power against which men make a

revolution, it must necessarily have rendered the great mass of humanity "propertyless," and produced, at the same time, the contradiction of an existing world of wealth and culture, both of which conditions presuppose a great increase in productive power, a high degree of its development. And, on the other hand, this development of productive forces . . . is absolutely necessary as a practical premise: firstly, for the reason that without it only *want* is made general, and with want the struggle for necessities and all the old filthy business would necessarily be reproduced.[1]

Marx's thesis is echoed in Michael Harrington's book *Socialism.* According to Harrington, the socialist vision is of an utterly new society. "Its most basic premise is that man's battle with nature has been completely won and there is therefore more than enough of material goods for everyone." [2] Harrington concludes that if abundance is not possible throughout the world, then neither is the socialist vision, because the divisive competition for scarce resources would remain. A truly new social order of brotherhood demands as a material precondition that there be enough for everyone.[3]

The sustainable society and the socialist vision drawn by Harrington do not coincide at all points, but both are material visions of the future and they have many similarities. Both call for and depend on a reduction of competitive pressures and an increase in cooperation, fraternity, and equality. Thus, for example, Harrington can further observe that while socialist values would be quite relevant to a spaceship economy, socialist emancipation of the personality would not be possible without abundance.[4]

Harrington's conclusions imply that only a repressive solution and continued "estrangement" are possible in

the sustainable society, unless, of course, it is characterized by high levels of material abundance. But high
levels of material abundance seem to be out of the
question if the futurists are correct and world population
remains at present levels.

Harrington's assessment may be accurate in view of
the many past conflicts over scarce resources. Unfortunately, like most pessimistic assessments, it seems to leave
no way out except economic collapse on the one hand
and a repressive society on the other.

Economist Robert L. Heilbroner takes a stance that
both agrees and disagrees with the futurists. He concurs
with the futurists as to the ultimate destination. He
agrees that the transition is critical, that some sort of
action is warranted, and that solutions require more than
the juggling of new technologies. But here he parts
company with the futurists. He feels that the period of
grace before limits are reached is considerably greater
than they project. He also has a much stronger faith in
the technological "fix," even though he admits that it will
not in the end avoid the need for the equilibrium
economy. Ultimately he is most pessimistic about the
possibility of rapid social change and criticizes the
futurists for naïveté in advocating the sustainable society.
We simply do not have the willingness to make sacrifices
for our unborn progeny, argues Heilbroner. Most of us
care very little about coming generations, a fact demonstrated by our lack of concern for our own generation.
At the start, therefore, we are faced with a lack of will.
Furthermore, there are the problems of knowing how to
motivate large numbers, how to deal with technical
complexities, and how to manipulate the social system

while avoiding totalitarian impositions. Concludes Heilbroner:

> It is clear that the imposition of such a program is far beyond our existing political and social capabilities. . . .
>
> The problem evaded by the anti-growth school . . . is how to mobilize the social will. . . . If we are to mount a response on the scale they propose, I suspect there is only one way—by the ghastly appearance of the initial stages of ecological disaster itself. . . . Short of such terrible stimuli, I do not believe that the pace of industrial growth will be significantly slowed. . . . Thus if, in the end, I pin my faith on "technology" . . . it is because I cannot think of anything today that is more likely to be useful in the solution of the problem that one day mankind will have to solve. . . .
>
> More sanguine than they about the technological possibilities of continuing industrial growth for a considerable period, I am far more pessimistic about the ease with which such a social transition can be made.[5]

One does not have to be an inveterate pessimist to appreciate Heilbroner's position concerning the social transition. The required technical, political, and ethical changes are staggering. Imagine, for example, a political leader taking a unilateral step to place severe limits on the growth process. The immediate effects would include a drop in interest rates, a consequent outflow of capital seeking a more profitable environment, a falling stock market, and unemployment. What leader could withstand the resulting pressures? Indeed, asks Heilbroner:

> Is this imaginable within a capitalist setting—that is, in a nation in which the business ideology permeates the views of nearly all groups and classes, and establishes the bounds of what is possible and natural, and what is not? Ordinarily I

do not see how such a question could be answered in any way but negatively, for it is tantamount to asking a dominant class to acquiesce in the elimination of the very activities that sustain it.[6]

If this is not enough, consider the complexities of working simultaneously with the many variables involved, each with a multitude of contributing variables. The modern technical society is a vast web of interrelated factors that simply will not yield to quick change or easy manipulation. And, to make matters still worse, the problems of each society are multiplied when the international context is introduced.

Booby Traps

As we have repeatedly attempted to point out, the thrust for growth is much too strong to be easily deflected. The present growth-oriented economic system is a well-oiled machine with a vague but nonetheless powerful supporting ideology. In spite of all the criticism of the present system, disaffection with its basic operation is not yet sufficient to produce significant change. Change will probably occur only when the gap between economic reality and social values is sufficiently wide to produce conflict. Today, however, there is far more consistency than conflict. In fact, the dominant value system is one in which the needs of the economic system play the most important role. The dominant values are largely determined by economic and technological considerations.

The gap between social values and economic reality obviously could widen through a change in social values. This gap is actually occurring. It is, as we have seen, the basis of the growth debate itself, which largely revolves around ideological and ethical issues. There would be no debate if a few had not opposed the growth ethos with a different set of values. But is this change in values occurring fast enough or with sufficient strength to influence the transition before limits are reached? We don't know, but available evidence suggests a negative answer, even though we hold out hope for a faster rate of change.

This negative conclusion is predicated in part on a disposition to side with Marx in his contention that economic factors dominate ideas in social change. This is not to say, as some Marxists do, that economic relationships are always the controlling factor—only that they seem to be in this case. The gap-producing change is more likely to come from the economic side, due to the strength of economic and technical factors in the current cultural synthesis.

At present there seems to be little in the way of gap-producing change coming from the economic side. The increasing number of those who advocate a sustainable society may reflect a change that is already occurring. But this seems unlikely. Rather, the changing attitudes are better seen as an increasing awareness of the inadequacies of the present growth ethic. They are not strong enough to signal a change in the economic base itself.

The present economic base is not static. But the change that is occurring seems to be much greater in the direction of more undifferentiated growth. Nor does there seem to be much in sight other than the appearance of limits to growth to alter this direction. The forces working to produce a change in values are simply not strong enough in the short run to overcome the thrust of the economic system. Hence Heilbroner opts for the technological solution as the best bet in a bad situation, for it alone of the alternatives does not require significant social change. Our best hope, according to Heilbroner, lies in the technological process pushing back limits long enough for new attitudes to develop. With this solution, however, comes the continued dominance of economic and technical power.

There are indeed many booby traps on the way to the sustainable society: wars over scarce resources, nuclear war, the tendency among human beings to exploit every situation for their own gain, and the real possibility of a repressive feudal solution. Even the optimistic authors of "A Blueprint for Survival" observe that "at times of great distress and social chaos, it is more than probable that governments will fall into the hands of reckless and unscrupulous elements, who will not hesitate to threaten neighboring governments with attack, if they feel that they can wrest from them a larger share of the world's vanishing resources." [7]

Yet There Is Hope

Should all these factors cause Christians to respond with pessimism? By no means! Even if subsequent events prove our hopes unfounded, to respond with pessimism ahead of time is pragmatically foolish. It cuts the ethical cord by eliminating positive choice. Moreover, pessimism can never be the stance of one who believes that God is at work in the world. Pessimism is the stance of one who has lost real hope. For the person who trusts in God's work of love, hope is never lost. But neither should we be optimistic.

It is necessary in this context to distinguish between hope and optimism, realism and pessimism. Realism can be distinguished from pessimism in that while both emphasize the factors in human existence that offer resistance to the realization of goals, realism can be maintained without losing the element of hope. One can be realistic about human pride and self-centeredness without turning them into a determinism. The consistent pessimist sees no way out, nothing to motivate behavior to seek even realizable goals.

If pessimism should be ruled out, then so also should optimism. The factors that offer resistance to the realization of the sustainable society are at present too overwhelming to allow optimism. In the face of these factors, optimism can lead only to disillusion and perhaps despair. Hope, however, is not synonymous with optimism. Hope is possible even when empirical signs point in the opposite·direction. Its basis is not the bright side of empirical evidence, but the assurance that God is at work, that light may at any moment shine in darkness.

Where is God at work? Where might he be at work in the future? Where might we find some signs of hope to balance our realism? Heilbroner himself points to one possibility.

In becoming aware of the hitherto unsuspected existence of a crucial environmental challenge, we feel within ourselves the first stirrings of an unaccustomed view of the human future, and of our responsibility for assuring that there will be a human future. Our generation is unlikely to solve the technical problems that will guarantee the indefinite viability of the planet, and will surely not solve the social challenges that are indissolubly associated with mankind's survival. But in the startled recognition that an ultimate ecological problem exists, it can set the stage for more decisive action by generations to follow.[8]

Thus Heilbroner's hope is that the trees planted now in the form of a new awareness of the future will bear fruit in the minds of our progeny. This suggests the continued twofold task of formulating new visions and alternative structures. Together these visions and structures prepare the way for new attitudes; they make plans available that can be implemented when the time is ripe. This twofold task is crucial, for once equilibrium is perceived as a necessity, the question will be whether the material-economic basis of our system can be changed quickly enough to avert overshoot and collapse. If an alternative ethic is available and the foundations for new institutions are prepared in advance, the transition will go more quickly and smoothly.

Beyond this hopefulness some ground even exists for a cautious optimism. Warning signs may well appear in advance of limits. As the M.I.T. study suggests,[9] a series of small crises may be encountered as limits are approached. Overshoot will not occur simultaneously in all places. Alternatively, especially in the case of nonrenewable resources, rising prices will probably offer a fairly reliable clue, if the causes of rising prices are known. In fact, equilibrium may not be imposed through overshoot and collapse, but by a gradual petering-out process brought on by sharply rising prices. These signals may well be a sufficient warning to avert much larger catastrophes and to create an atmosphere in which equilibrium is perceived as the only positive alternative. Indeed, the present rapid inflation in many parts of the world and the increasing competition for energy resources may be just such signals.

Furthermore, there are ample historical precedents of divided peoples and classes coming together to form a common front and make equal sacrifices in times of emergency. There is no *a priori* reason to expect that the crisis brought on by limits will lead to war, class conflict, or the exclusive pursuit of self-interest. Persons will undergo great discomfort, frustration, and discontinuity quite willingly if a crisis is perceived and there is a sense of working toward some meaningful end.

Periods of war offer the best examples. Wars are crises that frequently bring people together around a common purpose. Social pathology declines. Mental illness, anomie, and even suicide decrease.[10] In World War II there was widespread acceptance in the United States of the government's effort to ration meat to avoid the inequalities of the free market's distribution.[11]

World War II also provides some interesting examples of efforts along the lines of equilibrium.

> The "conservation of raw materials" received great emphasis; the federal government assumed the authority to allocate raw materials and ration essential goods; deliberate efforts were made to develop and utilize substitute materials. Millions of people salvaged newspapers, cans, and scrap iron, went without gasoline, planted victory gardens, and accepted substitutes for familiar products. Government and people were doing some of the kinds of things that might well be required in a society that was determined to cope with a serious environmental crisis.[12]

Nor can we overlook the fact that the most significant redistribution of income in recent times occurred in World War II.[13]

War may not be analogous to the sort of crisis that

limits may impose. The sacrifices asked for and made in World War II proceeded out of a sense of extreme emergency; a clear notion of who the enemy was; and assumptions that the crisis was to be short-lived, that we would win, and that afterward we would return to a more normal existence.

The environmental crisis may be different in many respects. The crisis will probably not be short-lived. There is no assurance of "victory." Normal existence, as defined by a growth economy and ethic, will not return. Finally, the enemy is not so well defined. Even so, the sense of extreme emergency is clearly the most important of these factors, perhaps in itself strong enough to motivate a common effort.

We should also be aware of the changing consciousness already taking place. A change of consciousness by a few will hardly reverse the scales in the absence of change in economic relationships. Nevertheless, idea and value changes do have an effect. Steps are now being taken to reduce pollution levels. The supersonic transport was voted down in large measure on environmental grounds. Increasingly, lawsuits and action by the Environmental Protection Agency are having small impacts.

Perhaps more significantly, new life-styles, communal living with an environmental awareness, and other small-scale experiments are offering individuals partial alternatives to the growth ethic. These experiments not only give individuals a new context of meaning and fulfillment, they also are testing grounds for possible styles of life in the sustainable society and counters to the growth ethic.

In all of this, certain pitfalls are present, the avoidance of which can enhance the chances of a successful transition. For example, consensus, equality of sacrifice, and a sense of common sharing will be essential. Nothing is more likely to destroy consensus and sharing than the notion that I am doing all the sacrificing while others are reaping benefits.

Moreover, too-frequent cries of "Wolf" can swamp us with urgency. Bombarded by an overload of crisis rhetoric, we often respond with apathy, withdrawal, or disbelief. Appeals to impending catastrophe will hardly by themselves stimulate consensus and cooperation. At best they produce a mentality of "muddling through." At worst they lead to pessimism, cynicism, and despair. Hence, to balance the specter of counterutopias there must be the alternative of a positive vision, a way out, a "can win" solution. Otherwise, we have little incentive to share and to create new possibilities. We think of survival only when our backs are against the wall. It is the condition out of which tyrants are born. In short, creative use of emergencies is greatly enhanced by a sense of positive purpose and all but eliminated if hope is tied to what is threatened with destruction.

We Are Not Alone

But where really are we to find a firm basis for hope? The pessimist easily rebuts even this guarded optimism. We also know that God is judge and that his wrath will descend on our pride, on our refusal to treat our neighbors justly, and on our continuing exploitation of the environment. Nevertheless, Christians also know God as Redeemer; as the one who is merciful beyond judgment; as the one who works through love to overcome pride and sloth.

It is this assurance that God is Redeemer upon which our hopes ultimately rest. We believe that God's love and our response will provide the resources to overcome the forces of destruction even in the most threatening situations. This does not mean a future of cornucopian abundance. Nor does it mean that we can sit back and let God do it. God simply doesn't work that way. We are free, free to affirm or deny Christ's lordship. God does not intervene like the Lone Ranger or Superman to reconcile what our denial of him has alienated. God's mercy and love are effective in persons and communities only with confession, repentance, and acceptance of new life. God now calls us to repentance and new direction. His call is to throw off the determinism of the past and the rigid, encrusted structures of the present. His call is to an open future where we can be assured he will be present.

In the context of our present discussion, this call is to three tasks: (1) to slow down and redirect the present narrow thrust for growth; (2) to determine our economic goals in terms of environmental soundness and human welfare and to act responsibly on this decision; (3) to make the possibilities of the future imaginatively concrete. We should have no illusions about bringing in the perfect society. Alienation will continue. Freedom and creativity will be tested to their limits. Problems will abound. Nonetheless, the call is clear. We are called to use our limited freedom and imagination in loving response to the love of God, not to become mired in the problems and to lose sight of the possibilities.

We affirm that the future is full of possibilities and hope. Some may despair at the prospects. Others may choose to escape into easy answers, strange cults, or simply into sloth. In contrast to despair and escape, the faithful response is a new spurt of creative imagination, a new effort to pull concrete possibilities out of an open future. Without vision there is little hope for higher levels of love, justice, and fulfillment.

The sustainable society is much more than a proposal to avoid catastrophe. Given certain qualifications, it is the vision we need to overcome injustice to persons and insensitivity to nature. For the church it may even be the opportunity to break its present affair with mammon and to review its commitment to persons, nature, and God. For humanists and Christians alike the new society could provide the occasion for dealing with a number of ethical problems now ignored in our single-minded pursuit of growth.

The sustainable society is not a bleak last resort or a bad vision challenging our hard-won material security. Our forefathers managed to survive without great abundance, and we have the enviable advantage of several centuries of discovery and invention. We are not headed back into the Dark Ages. Invention and discovery will not end with the thrust for growth. The sustainable society is a viable and even desirable alternative to the present growth economy and ethic.

Seeing the sustainable society as a positive possibility significantly enlarges the question, Is growth desirable? The sustainable society offers a new alternative, given three critical provisions: (1) the availability of basic material necessities to all; (2) a far more equitable distribution both internationally and domestically; and (3) a political process characterized by openness and not by repression. Now the question of desirability can be stated as a choice between growth and equilibrium. No longer need we ask whether growth is desirable or undesirable, but which is more desirable, a growth economy and ethic such as we have now with first-aid modifications, or the sustainable society?

To complete our discussion an answer to this question and the reasons for it are in order. In view of the costs of and limits to growth, the sustainable society may be necessary. But more important, in view of its positive possibilities, the sustainable society is desirable regardless of necessity. Put differently: on the grounds of both necessity and desirability, the sustainable society is the better choice.

Concretely this choice means an immediate move toward equilibrium within the more industrialized countries. For the less industrialized countries it means following suit as soon as significant strides have been made toward the elimination of poverty. Problematic in this choice is the question of who will be the carrier of the new ethic and the driving force behind the new economy. Without wishing to beg the issue, we can only say that the "who" is not yet apparent, for no clear and distinct group has emerged except a small number of futurists.

A New Vision

The sustainable society, rich and robust with human creativity and imagination, is our vision. We have just passed through a period that called itself realistic. Reinhold Niebuhr, for example, taught us well about the limitations of man and history, the dangers of "hard" and "soft" utopians. But Niebuhr never let the limitations be an excuse for moral inaction. Always for Niebuhr the limitations stood as a challenge, because he knew God as the Redeemer at the same time he understood the limitations of man and history. God at work to make life more tolerable and human: this was the vision that moved Niebuhr to moral action.

We desperately need the vision that moved Niebuhr, in his day, beyond realism. Yet we need it in a form that makes sense of present realities. The sustainable society provides such a vision. It is worth our responsible effort.

But we are adrift. Blown first toward illusion, then toward apathy and despair, we are without direction. This drift must stop, for the problems are great and God is already at work. God is calling us to stop our drift, to accept his redemptive activity, and to respond to the challenge presented by both the problems and the promises. This is not just empty exhortation. The problems are serious and require our best efforts. The promise assures us that we do not labor alone. Our frail craft, buffeted as it is by high winds and heavy seas, must stop its drift.

Problems and promises: we have enough of each to be realistic without despair, hopeful without illusion. Both the problems and the promises challenge us. The promises call us to find just and creative solutions to the problems. The problems push us to the limits of our ability to respond, taxing our imagination, creativity, and compassion. We are realistic because we know the past, but even more we are hopeful because we are sure of the future.

Notes

CHAPTER 1
THE GROWTH DEBATE

1. Jacques Ellul, *The Technological Society,* tr. by John Wilkinson (Vintage Books, Inc., 1964), p. xxv.

2. Edward F. Denison, "United States Economic Growth," in Peter M. Gutmann (ed.), *Economic Growth: An American Problem* (Prentice-Hall, Inc., 1964), pp. 84–100.

3. World Council of Churches, "Report: Science and Technology for Human Development," *Anticipation,* No. 19 (Nov. 1974), p. 17.

4. "Is Growth Obsolete?" James Tobin and William Nordhaus, *Economic Growth* (National Bureau of Economic Research, Inc., 1972).

5. Charles Elliott, *The Development Debate* (London: SCM Press Ltd., 1971), Ch. 3.

CHAPTER 2
CUSTODIANS AND CRITICS OF GROWTH

1. John F. Kennedy, address to the Yale University Class of 1962, *Yale Alumni Magazine,* July 1962, pp. 6–10.

2. K. William Kapp, *The Social Costs of Private Enterprise* (1950; Schocken Books, Inc., 1971).

3. Rachel Carson, *Silent Spring* (Houghton Mifflin Company, 1962).

4. Ezra J. Mishan, *The Costs of Economic Growth* (Frederick A. Praeger, Inc., Publishers, 1967).

5. Barry Commoner, *The Closing Circle* (Alfred A. Knopf, Inc., 1971), Ch. 9.

6. Kenneth Boulding, "Economics of the Coming Spaceship Earth," in Garrett De Bell (ed.), *The Environmental Handbook* (Ballantine Books, Inc., 1970), pp. 96–101.

7. Herman E. Daly, "Toward a Stationary-State Economy," in John Harte and Robert H. Socolow *et al., The Patient Earth* (Holt, Rinehart & Winston, Inc., 1971), pp. 226–244.

8. Jay W. Forrester, *World Dynamics* (Wright-Allen Press, Inc., 1971); Donella H. Meadows *et al., The Limits to Growth: A Report for the Club of Rome's Project on the Predicament of Mankind* (Universe Books, Inc., 1972).

9. "A Blueprint for Survival," *The Ecologist*, Vol. 2, No. 1 (Jan. 1972). Also see E. F. Schumacher, *Small Is Beautiful: A Study of Economics as If People Mattered* (Harper & Row, Publishers, Inc., 1974).

10. Harold J. Barnett and Chandler Morse, *Scarcity and Growth: The Economics of Natural Resource Availability* (The Johns Hopkins Press, 1963), Part I.

11. H. Paul Santmire, *Brother Earth: Nature, God, and Ecology in Time of Crisis* (Thomas Nelson, Inc., 1970), Chs. 1 and 2.

12. Anthony Crosland, *Fabian Tract 404: A Social Democratic Britain* (The Fabian Society, 11 Dartmouth St., London SW 1, 1971), pp. 5 f.

13. Gibson Winter, *Being Free: Reflections on America's Cultural Revolution* (The Macmillan Company, 1970), p. 104.

14. André Dumas, "The Ideological Factor in the West," in Egbert de Vries (ed.), *Man in Community: Christian Concern for the Human in Changing Society* (Association Press, 1966), pp. 71 f.

15. Victor C. Ferkiss, *Technological Man: The Myth and the Reality* (New American Library, 1969), pp. 35 f.

16. Philip E. Slater, *The Pursuit of Loneliness: American Culture at the Breaking Point* (Beacon Press, 1970), pp. 44 f.

17. Robert L. Heilbroner, *An Inquiry Into the Human Prospect* (W. W. Norton & Company, Inc., 1974), pp. 76–77.

18. Harvey G. Cox, *The Secular City: Secularization and Urbanization in Theological Perspective* (The Macmillan Company, 1964). In later writings Cox has moved away from a position that implicitly legitimates this synthesis. Also, Herbert W. Richardson, *Toward an American Theology* (Harper & Row, Publishers, Inc., 1967), especially Chs. 1–3.

19. John Kenneth Galbraith, *The New Industrial State* (The New American Library, 1967), Chs. 13–15.

CHAPTER 3
THE THRUST FOR GROWTH

1. Joseph Schumpeter, as quoted by Paul W. McCracken, "The Mainsprings of Economic Progress," in Laurence J. De Rycke (ed.), *Beginning Readings in Economics* (Council for Advancement of Secondary Education, 1961), p. 102.

2. Dennis Gabor, "Innovations Must Go On," *The New York Times,* Nov. 7, 1971.

3. W. Allen Wallis, "United States Growth: What, Why, How," in Edmund S. Phelps (ed.), *The Goal of Economic Growth,* rev. ed. (W. W. Norton & Company, Inc., 1969), p. 64.

4. Lester C. Thurow, "Research, Technical Progress, and Economic Growth," *Technology Review,* March 1971, p. 49.

5. Robert M. Solow, "Fixed Investment and Economic Growth," in Phelps (ed.), *The Goal of Economic Growth,* p. 91.

6. Edward F. Denison, "United States Economic Growth," in Gutmann (ed.), *Economic Growth,* pp. 84–100. For further discussion, see Gutmann (ed.), *Economic Growth,* pp. 31 ff., and Edward Shapiro, *Macroeconomic Analysis,* 2d ed. (Harcourt, Brace & World, Inc., 1970), pp. 461 ff. Tabular summaries can be found in the Denison essay and in the discussion in Shapiro. Denison includes many more factors in his analysis than these five. For purposes of simplification, however, they can be reduced to these categories.

7. Denison, "United States Economic Growth," in Gutmann (ed.), *Economic Growth,* p. 93.

8. Shapiro, *Macroeconomic Analysis,* p. 472.

9. Adam Smith, *Wealth of Nations,* Book I, Ch. 8.

10. Walter A. Weisskopf, *Alienation and Economics* (E. P. Dutton & Co., Inc., 1971), Chs. 2 and 3.

11. *Ibid.,* p. 90.

12. *Ibid.,* pp. 106–108.

13. Ironically, this ideology has competition. There is no logical reason for the consumption ethos and the requirements of economic and technological growth to dominate this relativistic and subjectivistic theory. The relativism and subjectivism of the theory might just as well be embodied in the antithesis of consumerism. Indeed, this is happening.

14. *Economic Report of the President* (U.S. Government Printing Office, 1973), p. 220.

15. Joint Economic Committee, Congress of the United States, *Staff Report on Employment, Growth, and Price Levels* (U.S. Government Printing Office, 1960), p. 43.

16. Weisskopf, *Alienation and Economics,* p. 174.

17. Slater, *The Pursuit of Loneliness,* pp. 133 f.

18. Ellul, *The Technological Society,* pp. 406 f.

19. Galbraith, *The New Industrial State,* p. 211.

20. *Ibid.,* p. 215.

21. Yale Brozen, "No 'Scarlet Letters': Advertising Has Come Under Dangerous and Unfair Attack," *The New York Times,* March 3, 1972, p. 53.

22. Eugene S. Schwartz, *Overskill: The Decline of Technology in Modern Civilization* (Ballantine Books, Inc., 1971), p. 13.

23. The debate between Lynn White, Jr., and his critics has attracted considerable attention and is of great importance to Christian theology and ethics. Though the debate is complex, in essence it points to the degree to which Western Christianity has neglected nature. For a fuller treatment of this debate, see my unpublished doctoral dissertation, *The Economic Growth Debate: A Christian Ethical Perspective* (unpublished doctoral dissertation, Columbia University, 1973), Ch. 3 and Appendix I. Also see: Lynn White, Jr., "The Historical Roots of Our Ecologic Crisis," *Science,* Vol. 155, No. 3767 (March 10, 1967), pp. 1203–1207; W. Lee Humphreys, "Pitfalls and Promises of Biblical Texts," in Glenn C. Stone (ed.), *A New Ethic for a New Earth* (Friendship Press, 1971), pp. 99–118; Cyril Richardson,

"A Christian Approach to Ecology," *Religion in Life,* Vol. 41, No. 4 (Winter 1972), pp. 462–479; Frederick Elder, *Crisis in Eden: A Religious Study of Man and Environment* (Abingdon Press, 1970); Thomas S. Derr, *Ecology and Human Need* (The Westminster Press, 1975).

24. Paul W. McCracken, "The Mainsprings of Economic Progress," in De Rycke (ed.), *Beginning Readings in Economics,* p. 99.

25. W. Allen Wallis, "A Philosophy of Economic Growth," in De Rycke (ed.), *Beginning Readings in Economics,* p. 302.

26. Robert A. Nisbet, *Social Change and History: Aspects of the Western Theory of Development* (Oxford University Press, 1969), p. 7.

27. Schwartz, *Overskill,* p. 59.

28. André Dumas, "The Ideological Factor in the West," in de Vries (ed.), *Man in Community,* p. 73.

29. Galbraith, *The New Industrial State,* p. 86.

30. *Ibid.,* p. 82.

31. *Ibid.,* p. 132.

32. *Ibid.,* Ch. 12.

33. *Ibid.,* p. 172.

34. *Ibid.,* p. 169.

35. *Ibid.,* p. 173.

36. *Ibid.,* p. 174.

37. *Ibid.,* p. 184.

38. Richard R. Nelson, "Technological Advance, Economic Growth, and Public Policy," in Walter W. Heller (ed.), *Perspectives on Economic Growth* (Random House, Inc., Vintage Books, 1968), p. 200.

CHAPTER 4
The Costs and Benefits of Growth

1. John Maynard Keynes, "Economic Possibilities for Our Grandchildren," in Phelps (ed.), *The Goal of Economic Growth,* p. 214.

2. Commoner, *The Closing Circle,* p. 46.

3. Gutmann, in Gutmann (ed.), *Economic Growth,* p. 7.

4. Kapp, *The Social Costs of Private Enterprise,* pp. 299 f.; also, Introduction and Ch. 1.

5. Commoner is aware that efficiency in relation to production is not the same as efficiency in relation to pollution. Frequently what increases industrial productivity decreases ecological productivity. The key to Commoner's position is the word "disproportionate." That is, a 42 percent increase of population does not account for the much larger increase of pollution. But, strangely enough, Commoner (*The Closing Circle,* p. 133) seems to overlook the fact that disproportionate pollution increases partially attributable to population might have resulted from sources other than obsolete factories. For example, the need to feed 42 percent more people *might* have been a significant additional pressure leading to the use of chemical fertilizers that pollute streams and lakes as per Commoner's own examples in his chapter "Illinois Earth" (*The Closing Circle,* Ch. 5). However, he seems to prefer to attribute the pollution caused by fertilizers to technological oversight rather than to population pressures. And here we encounter an example of Commoner's tendency to separate interrelated phenomena.

6. It is indicative of how little we know about pollution levels that Commoner is forced to estimate their increase as between 200 and 2,000 percent.

7. Commoner is, of course, correct. Economic growth can have a negative, neutral, or positive effect on the environment. Nevertheless, if economic growth is considered in broader terms as the thrust for growth, then there is a relation between it and environmental pollution. The heavy stress on growth to the exclusion of other considerations has been one of the primary factors leading to the myopia involved in undifferentiated growth. Commoner does not adequately deal with the relationships between "affluence" and environmentally degrading technologies. He divorces them in much the same way that he divorces population from technology. Economic growth (GNP per capita) and technological growth are closely related, as this study has repeatedly sought to demonstrate.

8. From Commoner, *The Closing Circle,* p. 143. Commoner has rejected "affluence" as a cause. Yet if you consider the list, at least some of the items would seem to be related to the desire to live well—for example, air conditioners, plastics,

electric housewares, electric power, and motor fuel. In view of this, it would again seem that Commoner has offered a too narrow definition of "affluence."

9. Commoner, *The Closing Circle,* p. 177.

10. *Ibid.,* p. 266.

11. *Ibid.,* p. 268.

CHAPTER 5
THREE ETHICAL ISSUES

1. According to U.S. Census Bureau statistician Herman P. Miller (*Rich Man, Poor Man* [Thomas Y. Crowell Company, 1971], p. 16), income distribution in 1966 was as follows, in terms of fifths from lowest income to highest: the lowest fifth of families and individuals received 5 percent of the income, while the second fifth received 11 percent, the middle fifth received 18 percent, the fourth fifth received 23 percent, and the highest fifth received 43 percent of all the income. The percentage of the income received by all segments varied only slightly after taxes. The imbalance of income received is further shown by other figures from 1966, according to which the top 5 percent of families received 14 percent of all the income, and the top 1 percent received 5 percent of the income. Little if any shift has occurred in U.S. income-distribution figures since World War II.

The distribution of wealth (rather than annual income) is more skewed. According to figures cited by Miller (p. 157), the distribution of wealth owned in the United States in 1962 was as follows: Of the total of consumer units (i.e., families of two or more persons and independent individuals), the bottom 25 percent held less than ½ of 1 percent of the wealth. The next 35 percent held 7 percent of the wealth. The next 23 percent held 18 percent of the wealth. The next 11 percent held 18 percent of the wealth. And the top 6 percent held 57 percent of the wealth. The imbalance of wealth owned is shown also by figures from 1968: just 1.2 percent of the total— or 700,000 families and individuals—held 35 percent of the wealth.

Available evidence suggests that wealth differentials are increasing. The question usually asked at this point is, How can all this be possible with supposedly "confiscatory" taxation, a progressive income tax, and various welfare programs? The reasons are not difficult to find. According to sociologists S. M. Miller and Martin Rein ("Can Income Redistribution Work?" *Social Policy,* Vol. 6, No. 1 [May–June 1975], pp. 3–18), the overall tax system in fact is not progressive. The distribution of income and wealth before and after taxes and welfare transfers is nearly the same. Contrary to popular wisdom Miller and Rein conclude: "American and British experiences are surprisingly convergent in showing greater inequality in the distribution of nontransfer income; an increase in recent years in the scope and redistributive effects of public programs; but that the net effect was to leave the final distribution of income much the same."

2. Robert Lampman, "Perspectives on Growth," in Heller (ed.), *Perspectives on Economic Growth,* pp. 158–160.

3. J. R. Hicks, "Growth and Anti-Growth," *Oxford Economic Papers,* Nov. 1966, p. 264.

4. Crosland, *Fabian Tract 404,* p. 3.

5. Consider what Philip M. Stern has called "Uncle Sam's Welfare Program—For the Rich" (*The New York Times Magazine,* April 16, 1972). According to Stern, certain "tax savings" allowed particularly to the rich under our present tax structure ought to be considered as identical to that of a direct federal handout. Thus, when men like J. Paul Getty are excused from paying $70 million in taxes, the effect is the same as it would be if Mr. Getty were to receive a $70 million federal welfare check. Stern concludes from a Brookings Institution study under economists Joseph A. Pechman and Benjamin Okner that our present tax system excuses and thus "hands out" $77.3 billion in "welfare" payments of which "just $92 million goes to the six million poorest families in the nation, while 24 times that amount—82.2 billion—goes to just 3,000 families."

6. Paul Ramsey, *Basic Christian Ethics* (Charles Scribner's Sons, 1950), pp. 12 f.

7. Burton A. Weisbrod, "Collective Action and the Distribution of Income," in Robert H. Haveman and Julius Margolis (eds.), *Public Expenditures and Policy Analysis* (Markham Publishing Company, 1970), pp. 118–119.

8. Galbraith, *The New Industrial State*, p. 366.

9. Edwin G. Dolan, *TANSTAAFL: The Economic Strategy for Environmental Crisis* (Holt, Rinehart & Winston, Inc., 1971), pp. 41 f.

10. Barry Commoner, "The Meaning of the Environmental Crisis," address to the Environmental Forum, United Nations Conference on the Human Environment, Stockholm, Sweden, June 5, 1972.

11. For example, see: John R. Maddox, *The Doomsday Syndrome* (McGraw-Hill Book Co., Inc., 1972); Hans Landsberg, *Natural Resources for U.S. Growth: A Look Ahead to the Year 2000* (Johns Hopkins Press, 1964), especially Ch. 1; Barnett and Morse, *Scarcity and Growth*, especially pp. 246–251; Herman Kahn and B. Bruce-Briggs, *Things to Come: Thinking About the Seventies and Eighties* (The Macmillan Company, 1972).

12. Ethicist Roger Shinn has dealt with the continuum raised by optimistic and pessimistic assessments of the population problem. See Roger L. Shinn, "Ethics and the Family of Man," in Michael Hamilton (ed.), *This Little Planet* (Charles Scribner's Sons, 1970), pp. 148–152.

13. *Ibid.*, pp. 151 f.

14. As quoted in *ibid.*, p. 152.

CHAPTER 6
Is Growth Desirable?

1. Crosland, *Fabian Tract 404*, p. 5.

2. Richard Neuhaus, *In Defense of People: Ecology and the Seduction of Radicalism* (The Macmillan Company, 1971), pp. 116 f.

3. Barry Commoner, "The Meaning of the Environmental Crisis," address to the Environmental Forum, United Nations Conference on the Human Environment, Stockholm, Sweden, June 5, 1972.

4. *Ibid.*

CHAPTER 7
The Limits to Growth

1. "A Blueprint for Survival," *The Ecologist,* Vol. 2, No. 1 (Jan. 1972), p. 2.

2. Commoner, *The Closing Circle;* see pp. 232, 274, 295 f.

3. Jay W. Forrester, *World Dynamics* (Wright-Allen Press, Inc., 1971).

4. Donella H. Meadows *et al., The Limits to Growth* (Universe Books, Inc., 1972). The Club of Rome is an informal organization of thirty individuals from several fields and countries whose declared purpose is to foster understanding of the varied but interdependent components that make up the global system in which we all live.

5. Mihajlo Mesarovic and Eduard Pestel, *Mankind at the Turning Point: The Second Report to the Club of Rome* (Reader's Digest Press, 1974).

6. Meadows *et al., The Limits to Growth,* p. 63.

7. *Ibid.,* pp. 64–67.

8. *Ibid.,* pp. 84 ff.

9. *Ibid.,* p. 126.

10. Forrester, *World Dynamics,* pp. 74–80.

11. Mesarovic and Pestel, *Mankind at the Turning Point,* p. vii.

12. This insight brings into focus certain remarks by Barry Commoner to the Environmental Forum at the 1972 U.N. Conference on the Human Environment. Commoner scores the M.I.T. study for seeking solutions to the ecological crisis through the elimination of population and economic growth. Recalling his position from an earlier discussion that the crisis is primarily a result of specific polluting technologies undergirded by the quest for profits, Commoner claims that the M.I.T. team's conclusions fail to take account of these underlying economic factors and the negative impact of an equilibrium economy on the poor. He goes on to repeat his solution, i.e., that the underlying economic factors need to be altered and environmentally destructive innovations eliminated.

Commoner's criticism is not telling. In the first place, his economic analysis can easily be added to the M.I.T. study.

It adds a measure of depth, but it certainly does not change the picture much. The thrust for growth and the role of polluting and depleting technologies clearly lie behind the team's assumptions. Second, Commoner seems to think the team's call for the elimination of growth refers to all forms of growth. The team, however, is well aware that differentiated economic and technological growth is possible and that "affluence" itself is not the major culprit. Finally, although the social-ethical implications are not foremost in the M.I.T. study, they are mentioned (*The Limits to Growth,* pp. 178 ff.). Forrester, in particular, notes several that are consistent with Commoner's own observations.

In fact, Commoner seems to overlook the interrelatedness of factors, a strange oversight given his insistence (*The Closing Circle,* pp. 33 ff.) that "everything is connected to everything else." And while leverage on the ecological crisis is perhaps greatest at the point of polluting and depleting technologies, it would be wise for him to give greater scrutiny to the interrelationships explored in the M.I.T. study and not to rely so heavily on statistics. It is neither new technologies, nor economic forces, nor "affluence," nor population alone which is the problem, but the totality buttressed by ideological factors. Furthermore, to reduce it to one factor tends to negate gains realizable through a changed consciousness resulting from attacks made on a number of related problems.

13. Carl Kaysen, "The Computer That Printed Out Wolf," *Foreign Affairs,* Vol. 50, No. 4 (July 1972), pp. 660–668.

14. Martin Shubik, "Modeling on a Grand Scale," *Science,* Vol. 174, No. 4013 (Dec. 3, 1971), pp. 1014 f.

15. Peter Passell, Marc Roberts, and Leonard Ross, *The New York Times Book Review,* April 2, 1972, p. 1.

16. H. S. D. Cole *et al.* (eds.), *Models of Doom: A Critique of the Limits to Growth* (Universe Books, Inc.), 1973.

17. Kaysen, "The Computer That Printed Out Wolf," *loc. cit.,* pp. 664 f. The subtlety of the Kaysen criticism should not be missed. It is not so much a question of whether or not technology is growing exponentially. Rather, the problem might be in relative rates. Thus one could viably maintain that the technological process grows exponentially but at a lower

rate than the factors pressing against limits. Hence limits would still be reached even with exponentially growing technology. However, as Kaysen suggests, such a position would considerably reduce the possibility of collapse and lengthen the period of grace before limits are reached.

18. Meadows *et al., The Limits to Growth,* pp. 149 ff.

19. *Ibid.,* p. 154.

20. Mesarovic and Pestel, *Mankind at the Turning Point,* pp. 30 f. and Ch. 6.

CHAPTER 8
THE SUSTAINABLE SOCIETY

1. Meadows *et al., The Limits to Growth,* pp. 168 f.

2. "A Blueprint for Survival," *The Ecologist,* Vol. 2, No. 1 (Jan. 1972), pp. 8–22; Kenneth Boulding, "Fun and Games with the Gross National Product," in Harold W. Helfrich (ed.), *The Environmental Crisis: Man's Struggle to Live with Himself* (Yale University Press, 1970), pp. 157–170; John B. Cobb, Jr., *Is It Too Late? A Theology of Ecology* (Beverly Hills: Bruce Books, 1972), Ch. 7; Commoner, *The Closing Circle,* Chs. 11, 13; Herman E. Daly, "Toward a Stationary-State Economy," in Harte and Socolow, *The Patient Earth;* Herman E. Daly, *Toward a Steady-State Economy* (W. H. Freeman and Company, 1973); *Daedalus,* Fall 1973; Meadows *et al., The Limits to Growth,* Ch. 5; Mesarovic and Pestel, *Mankind at the Turning Point;* John Stuart Mill, *Principles of Political Economy,* Vol. II (London, 1857), pp. 320–326; World Council of Churches, "Report: Science and Technology for Human Development," *Anticipation,* No. 19 (Nov. 1974).

3. Meadows *et al., The Limits to Growth,* p. 171.

4. *Ibid.,* pp. 173 f.

5. Mesarovic and Pestel, *Mankind at the Turning Point,* p. 127.

6. Daly, "Toward a Stationary-State Economy," in Harte and Socolow, *The Patient Earth,* p. 231.

7. Schumacher, *Small Is Beautiful,* Parts I and II.

8. Samuel L. Parmar, "Ethical Guidelines and Social Options After the Limits to Growth Debate," *Anticipation,* No. 18 (Aug. 1974), pp. 20–23.

9. "A Blueprint for Survival," *The Ecologist,* Vol. 2, No. 1 (Jan. 1972), p. 14.

10. Herman E. Daly, *The Stationary-State Economy,* Distinguished Lecture Series, No. 2 (University of Alabama Graduate School of Business, 1971), p. 16.

11. Keynes, in Phelps (ed.), *The Goal of Economic Growth,* p. 210.

12. Schumacher, *Small Is Beautiful,* p. 145.

CHAPTER 9
PROBLEMS AND POSSIBILITIES

1. Karl Marx and Friedrich Engels, *The German Ideology,* ed. by R. Pascal (International Publishers Co., Inc., 1947), p. 24.

2. Michael Harrington, *Socialism* (Saturday Review Press, 1972), p. 344.

3. *Ibid.,* pp. 347, 351.

4. *Ibid.,* p. 347.

5. Robert L. Heilbroner, "Growth and Survival," *Foreign Affairs,* Vol. 51, No. 1 (Oct. 1972), pp. 150–152. Also see Heilbroner's even more pessimistic assessment, *An Inquiry Into the Human Prospect.*

6. Robert L. Heilbroner, *Between Capitalism and Socialism: Essays in Political Economics* (Random House, Inc., Vintage Books, 1970), p. 283.

7. "A Blueprint for Survival," *The Ecologist,* Vol. 2, No. 1 (Jan. 1972), p. 5.

8. Heilbroner, "Growth and Survival," *Foreign Affairs,* Vol. 51, No. 1 (Oct. 1972), p. 153. Heilbroner's work usually concludes on a hopeful note. Nevertheless, in his latest book *(An Inquiry Into the Human Prospect)* the hope is severely muted. As Heilbroner considers the problems involved, he seems to become more pessimistic.

9. Meadows *et al., The Limits to Growth,* p. 52.

10. Kenneth Keniston, *Youth and Dissent: The Rise of a New Opposition* (Harcourt Brace Jovanovich, Inc., 1971), p. 42.

11. James W. Kuhn and Ivar Berg, *Values in a Business Society* (Harcourt, Brace & World, Inc., 1968), p. 140.

12. John Rodman, "Ecopolis," lecture delivered to the

Conference on Alternatives to Catastrophe, School of Theology at Claremont, California, May 5, 1972.

13. Simon Kuznets, *Modern Economic Growth* (Yale University Press, 1966), p. 215.